PRAISE FOR *SCARY GOD*

"My friend Mattie Montgomery is a man who lives by his convictions and has a zeal to see the church live out its fullest potential. His new book *Scary God*, brings you face-to-face with our Warrior King God. Our God is not small, and He can do far more than we could ever imagine but too often we stay stuck with small mind-sets of who God is. This book will challenge you to live in a way that says my God is mighty and powerful!"

—JOHN BEVERE, BESTSELLING AUTHOR, SPEAKER, AND COFOUNDER OF MESSENGER INTERNATIONAL

"This book is like nothing I've ever read before about God or the subject of the fear of the Lord. Mattie does an amazing job of unraveling what the fear of God actually is and how the right way of fearing Him frees you from this world's bondage and from living your life on distant terms with God. I love that in this book he addresses many tough subjects and brings light to those shady gray areas many don't want to talk about. If you want to kill complacency, if you want to live free of the fear of man and discover the depths of God burning in your heart again, then you should definitely read this book."

—BEN FITZGERALD, SENIOR LEADER, AWAKENING EUROPE/ AWAKENING AUSTRALIA

"You do not want to mess with Mattie. Yes, Mattie *is* 'built.' But the reason you don't want to mess with Mattie is because his words come from God's Word. And the God Mattie serves? 'It is a fearful thing to fall into His hands' (Heb. 10:31). In *Scary God* Mattie wants the church to rightly quake in the Almighty's presence. Mattie's storytelling will slap you across the face and his stories will make you step back. *Scary God* will put you on your knees, not before Mattie but before the God Mattie and I serve 'with fear and trembling' (Phil. 2:12)."

—DR. MARK ECKEL, PRESIDI

"*Scary God.* I absolutely love this title for several reasons because *no one* is talking about the scariness of God anymore. We have domesticated an American Jesus whose primary aim is making us happy, and yet it's His unpredictability, His awesomeness, His holiness, His intensity that release trembling and holy fear back into the church and the earth. I wholeheartedly endorse this man, this book, and this message. I pray that God uses it to light a fire in the church, in the earth, and that the fear of the Lord and the love of God would be properly restored in this day."

—COREY RUSSELL, DIRECTOR OF THE FORERUNNER PROGRAM
AT THE INTERNATIONAL HOUSE OF PRAYER UNIVERSITY

"I'm so thankful for Mattie's heart and his desire to guide believers and nonbelievers alike toward understanding who God really is. This book will take you on a journey of dissecting scriptural truth to relinquish your preconceived notions of evil and discover genuine freedom from fear!"

—MATTY MULLINS, VOCALIST, MEMPHIS MAY FIRE

SCARY GOD

SCARY GOD

INTRODUCING THE FEAR OF THE LORD
TO THE POSTMODERN CHURCH

MATTIE MONTGOMERY

EMANATE
BOOKS

Published in Nashville, Tennessee, by Emanate Books, an imprint of Thomas Nelson. Emanate Books and Thomas Nelson are registered trademarks of HarperCollins Christian Publishing, Inc.

Thomas Nelson titles may be purchased in bulk for educational, business, fund-raising, or sales promotional use. For information, please e-mail SpecialMarkets@ThomasNelson.com.

Unless otherwise noted, Scripture quotations are taken from the New King James Version®. © 1982 by Thomas Nelson. Used by permission. All rights reserved.

Scripture quotations marked ESV are from the ESV® Bible (The Holy Bible, English Standard Version®). Copyright © 2001 by Crossway, a publishing ministry of Good News Publishers. Used by permission. All rights reserved.

Scripture quotations marked KJV are from the King James Version. Public domain.

Scripture quotations marked NASB are from New American Standard Bible®. Copyright © 1960, 1962, 1963, 1968, 1971, 1972, 1973, 1975, 1977, 1995 by The Lockman Foundation. Used by permission. (www.Lockman.org)

Scripture quotations marked NIV are from the Holy Bible, New International Version®, NIV®. Copyright © 1973, 1978, 1984, 2011 by Biblica, Inc.® Used by permission of Zondervan. All rights reserved worldwide. www.Zondervan.com. The "NIV" and "New International Version" are trademarks registered in the United States Patent and Trademark Office by Biblica, Inc.®

Italics in Scripture quotations have been added by author for emphasis.

ISBN 978-1-4002-0819-7 (eBook)

ISBN 978-1-4002-0818-0 (TP)

Library of Congress Control Number: 2018943313

Printed in the United States of America

18 19 20 21 22   LSC   10 9 8 7 6 5 4 3 2 1

This book is dedicated to all the seekers; young and old, rich and poor, near and far. Your hunger moves heaven, and your passion can change the world. May you find what you're looking for . . .

Let us hear the conclusion of the whole matter: Fear God and keep His commandments, for this is man's all.

—ECCLESIASTES 12:13

CONTENTS

INTRODUCTION

Brock the Bully

People tend not to mess with me much. Probably because I stand well over six feet tall and weigh more than two hundred pounds. The tattoos on my arms and neck may have something to do with it too. But it hasn't always been this way.

Before a high school junior year growth spurt, I was a bit of a shrimp. And shrimp tend to get eaten by bigger fish. At six years old, I was a scrawny brown kid with my hair parted down the middle, kicking around in some untied Reebok pump tennis shoes with holes in the knees of my jeans.

I may have been small for my age, but I felt big on the inside, convinced that I'd watched enough of the Teenage Mutant Ninja Turtles that I'd actually learned karate. Obviously, I spent a lot of my time in an imaginary world, riding my bike around the property of my Pacific Northwest apartment complex, looking for bad guys to bring to justice.

For better or worse, I found one.

Let's call him Brock. He was a slightly older, slightly less scrawny kid living somewhere on the other side of our small cluster of buildings.

His bike was bigger and faster than mine. His clothes were trendier: colorful cotton pants with a vertical zigzag pattern and elastic cuffs at the bottom. Oh, and slip-on skateboard shoes.

With his long, straight, dark-brown hair tucked back behind his ears, Brock was cooler, bigger, and tougher than I was. And for some reason, he didn't like me.

He singled me out for persecution. First I got pelted by pine cones when I rode by. Then he upped the attack, chasing after me and pushing me off my bike. He did all this in front of several of his friends, as if he were putting on a show and I was literally his fall guy.

Each time he'd pump up his pride by stealing some of mine, I'd burn with embarrassment and shame, swearing that I'd never let it happen again.

Desperate to avoid being humiliated, I'd try to keep out of Brock's way, riding around with eyes peeled and a knot in my stomach. When the ultimately unavoidable confrontation did occur, I'd flail my arms and attempt to fight back—though I am not sure he noticed.

I'd tell him to leave me alone, snarling in my toughest voice, but he did not seem to be intimidated. The muscles I liked to pretend I had didn't impress him. Nor did the martial arts poses I'd learned from repeated viewings of *The Karate Kid*.

Come to think of it, my riding a bike adorned with Mickey Mouse designs likely didn't help present much of a fearsome image either.

Anyway, after a few days of this public taunting, it became clear that my petitions for justice and threats of revenge were falling on deaf ears. And my typical optimism, which had up to this point persuaded me that *next time things will be different; just wait*, had begun to leak.

After being pushed off my bike yet again, I was forced to face a harsh reality: I simply didn't have what it took to stop Brock from picking on me. So, jettisoning the superhero playbook, I opted for the typical six-year-old response: I ran home and told my mom.

MY FIERCE FATHER

When I burst through the door with scraped, dirty knees, and tears in my eyes, Mom knew immediately what had happened. I'd been telling her for days about my new mortal enemy.

Each time I came home bloody and bruised, Mom would tend my scrapes and soothe my bruised ego. She would tell me not to worry, that Brock might not like me, but lots of other people did—and that she loved me. She would tell me to ignore him, to be nice to him, to avoid him, that he'd get tired of picking on me in time. You know, typical mom stuff.

Her affirming words and sympathy didn't solve anything, but they made me feel better for a while.

But this day she never got to dispense another dose of mom tonic. "Son!"

This was bellowed from the next room by my father, who had heard my defeated return home.

"Let's go," he thundered as he walked past me to the front door, purpose and conviction in every step.

Dad was about the size of a small mountain. A lineman for his football team in college, he stood over six feet tall, weighing 250 pounds. His round belly and broad shoulders constantly strained the limits of his tight-fitting T-shirts. A thick black beard and gold earring framed his round, chocolate-brown face and wild eyes. This was not a man to mess with.

I knew this from personal experience. When I was out of line, he would fix me with an intense look that told me my world was about to change. Now he had that same stern demeanor as he looked down at me and announced, "We'll handle this right now."

I thought he was going to kill Brock—and I was okay with it.

Dad opened the door and turned, motioning for me to follow. My heart was beating so violently in my chest I could feel it in my ears.

"Show me where he is," he instructed, setting out of our small apartment at a furious pace. With me doing a sort of jog/skip/power-walk to keep up with him, we quickly came to the courtyard in the middle of our apartment complex. There was Brock, still riding his bike around with two little lackeys, looking all smug and safe and self-absorbed. He had no idea what was coming for him.

To be honest, I was scared. I didn't remember ever having seen my father quite like this before, even when he was putting me straight. This was going to be the confrontation to end all confrontations. This would be Armageddon meets the Super Bowl meets Rocky versus Drago the Russian.

There was no talking, other than to confirm Dad's query, "He's the one in the stupid pants?" The earth itself seemed to shake with each determined step as he made a beeline across the courtyard toward Brock, my stubby legs churning as fast as possible trying to keep up with him.

Though my head came up only to my dad's waist, I stuck my chest out, trying to look brave. This was one fight, I thought, that I would have to let him handle. *And oh boy, he could handle it, all right.* Justice was on its way for Brock the bully, and its name was Dad!

About ten yards from the group of boys, my father thundered, "Brock!" I think his voice echoed a few times, and the earth may even have paused in its rotation for a moment, though that might just be my imagination. The boys all froze in their tracks as they stopped their bikes and turned to face him, eyes wide with horror.

Dad kept walking until he was right in front of my tormentor. Brock's head was bent all the way back, his mouth wide open in shock as he stood in the shadow of Mount Dad, trying to see the peak. My father slowly bent down until he was eye to eye with the bully. His face was still just as intense as when he'd stormed out of the apartment.

Then things took an unexpected turn. To my surprise, instead of knocking Brock into the next state, my dad reached back and grabbed me by the arm. He pulled me forward forcefully, into the conversation.

Without breaking eye contact with Brock, he said, "This is *my* son." He paused to make sure he'd been heard. Turning to me, he went on, "Son, if this boy puts his hands on you or any of your things ever again, you have my permission to knock his teeth out."

I swallowed, blinked, and nodded, trying to hide the fact that I was probably just as scared of him in that moment, and of what he'd just said, as Brock was. All I could think was, *This doesn't make much sense.* After all, Brock was much bigger than me, much stronger than me, and much tougher than me.

If I could have knocked Brock's teeth out, wouldn't I have already done so? Hadn't my dad just made everything worse? Was there any way that this would work? Why didn't he just rip one of Brock's arms off and beat him with it? That would have been so much simpler.

As my dad stood back up and surveyed the group of little boys he'd just thoroughly terrified, Brock and his two little friends held their breath and shook. I began to imagine the retribution I might suffer at Brock's hands for having ratted him out. I thought about the further mockery and bullying I was probably going to have to endure now.

My father turned and glanced at me one last time, and cracked his stern exterior with a sly smile as he walked back toward our apartment. I was still trembling from the excitement and adrenaline as I watched him turn around a corner and disappear out of sight.

I could feel Brock and his friends looking at me. I expected laughter or some sort of sneer, maybe even a threat, but there was nothing. Somehow finding the courage, I turned to face them. There was a brief tense moment of silence, a standoff, before one by one they climbed back onto their bikes and rode off.

Brock never said another word to me.

From that day on, I was fearless. I moved around that apartment complex as if I owned the place. I know I still wasn't the biggest, strongest, or toughest kid on the block. But I also knew that *no one* would mess with my dad—and that he would make sure no one messed with me.

CONFRONTING THE BROCKS

During my years in ministry, I have met countless Christians who are repeatedly being pushed off their bikes by their own Brocks. They are harassed and intimidated, exhausted and robbed by the things that hang around outside their front doors—and I think it's time for that to stop.

The reason I believe God has entrusted me with the message contained in *Scary God* is because He, like my earthly father, hates to see His children harassed. And He is more than able to handle anything and everything that has been harassing them.

The problem, though, is that many of us in the postmodern incarnation of the body of Christ don't actually believe that our Father can handle the bullies that harass us. We've forgotten who our Dad is, so we're spending our lives trying to run faster or fight harder, when decisive deliverance has been waiting in our Father's shadow all along.

The time has come for us, as the people of God, to remember who our heavenly Father is—to realize that He is bigger, stronger, and scarier than any of the threats that may have come against us, and to then start living like it.

As the famed nineteenth-century Baptist preacher Charles Spurgeon wrote, "The fear of God is the death of every other fear. Like a mighty lion, it chases all other fears [away]."[1] If we can lay hold of the true, pure fear of the Lord, then we will be able to let go of the false, contaminated fears that keep so many Christians muzzled, weak, and spiritually impotent. We've become slaves to the fear of man, the fear of failure, the fear of abandonment, the fear of vulnerability. Such fears have stolen the intended inheritance from many sons and daughters, and disqualified countless others from the full power and potency in which they were destined to live.

THE TIME HAS COME FOR US, AS THE PEOPLE OF GOD, TO REMEMBER WHO OUR HEAVENLY FATHER IS.

There is a world waiting desperately outside our churches for a people to emerge who walk with confidence in the might of their God. And they've been waiting for too long. Most of the world doesn't believe that our God is alive and powerful because most of the church lives as though He isn't.

My prayer for you as you walk with me through *Scary God* is that you will be left in awe as you see a side of your Father you may never even have imagined before. I want you to behold—maybe for the first time—the great Warrior King who calls you "beloved." My desire is that you will truly understand the fierceness, fire, and fullness of Yahweh, the Most High God and our great Champion. I hope that, upon completing this book, you will be able to echo, with greater confidence and conviction than ever before, the words of the apostle Paul in Romans 8:31, "If God is for [me], who can be against [me]?"

As part of all that, I'll invite you to join me in a prayer at the end of each chapter, asking God to seal what He may have shown you.

At the end of it all, my hope is that if Brock is ever foolish enough to come at you again, you will have the courage to face him down, knowing that your God is far scarier than your enemy, and that He loves you relentlessly.

Walking in the security and safety of the fear of the Lord, we can face any situation or circumstance with certainty, determination, and faith.

Let's Pray

Father,

I ask that You would prepare my heart for the message contained within these pages.

Humble me now in Your presence and deliver me from complacency, that I might seek You and know You the way I was created to, amen.

CHAPTER 1

FRIGHTENED TO LIFE

And now, Israel, what does the LORD *your God require*
of you, but to fear the LORD *your God, to walk in all*
His ways and to love Him, to serve the LORD *your*
God with all your heart and with all your soul.
—DEUTERONOMY 10:12

The first time God scared me was in a trailer in Virginia. Now, don't get me wrong. I'm not saying that He was unkind or that He assaulted or attacked me. It wasn't like in a horror movie, when someone suddenly appears at the window and everyone jumps out of their skin, hearts pounding.

He wasn't mean. He didn't frighten me for the sake of it. He simply let me experience more of Him than I ever had before. And it was scary!

I think I should say this early and clearly in this book: there is a difference between being scary and being mean. The risk in some teaching on the fear of the Lord is that people may be tempted to regard God as cruel and maniacal, when that couldn't be further from the truth.

Like any good father, He has a tremendous intensity and a capacity for violence—but these are driven not by uncontrollable rage or brutality, but by jealous love. The most frightening thing about God is simply how dramatically, indescribably different He is from any created thing.

When I had that encounter in Virginia, I wasn't unfamiliar with what Christians talk about as "the presence of the Lord." You may have experienced it yourself in a special worship gathering, or even in your own time with God—a sense of His closeness, His sweetness, His kindness. Like a warm blanket, comforting and safe.

Having grown up in church, I'd known many moments like that. I'd stood through countless worship services and prayer times. I'd cried at youth camp altar calls with my friends while the worship band played our favorite song. I'd stood for my faith at See You at the Pole rallies. I'd been grateful for God's gentle presence.

I'm not knocking such experiences at all. But they are nothing like what happened in that mobile home somewhere outside Virginia Beach.

Though I had a church heritage, by this stage of my life, I was spending more time in dingy, sweaty clubs than in bright, clean sanctuaries. With the best intentions, though.

In the fall of 2007, I had left everyone and everything I'd ever known to join For Today. I became the front man for this unheard-of metal band from western Iowa because I thought it would give me the chance to share the gospel with people who needed to hear it. I was right.

We were not very popular in those early days, but every night, during our set in some dark room somewhere, I'd preach the good news about Jesus, and every night the message would transform lives. It was exciting and fulfilling.

At each tour stop, we would hope and pray (and sometimes beg) for one of the few people attending that concert to be generous enough to let us sleep on the floor of their home. Sometimes we'd get no offers and end up parking our van and trailer in a truck-stop parking lot for the night. But often we'd make new friends, or connect with old ones, who would kindly inconvenience themselves to accommodate us.

Slogging our way through another seven-shows-a-week tour, we came to Virginia Beach in the summer of 2008. We'd played there a number of times before. After the concert, we met a local pastor who asked if we needed a place to stay for the night. We gladly (desperately) accepted his invitation.

He explained there was a mobile home on his church's property that had been converted into a prayer room. People may come in throughout the night to pray in one small section, he told us, but the rest of the trailer was separate, with couches and carpet on which we were more than welcome to spread out. Yes, thank you!

After packing all the instruments and gear into our trailer, we piled into our big purple van and followed the pastor's car to the church property. We arrived well after midnight. As we grabbed our sleeping bags and pillows and poured out of the sliding side door of the van, it seemed like just another one of oh-so-many such stops. We'd stumble into our temporary home to sleep for a few hours before waking up to leave and do it all over again.

But as I walked through the door of the trailer, the atmosphere of peace and stillness that seemed to rest in that place immediately struck me. Two lamps set on either side of the room cast a dim light that made the lounge feel sleepy. However, there was enough light for me to be able to tell that the brown carpet was nice and thick— something to which I paid special attention because I knew that's where I'd be sleeping.

We all spread out to claim our spots for the night—a couple on couches, the rest of us on the floor. After laying out my sleeping bag and pillow in one corner, I decided to spend some time in the small prayer room that was just on the other side of a thin wall.

Upon entering the prayer room, I noticed that one of the walls was coated in chalkboard paint, with prayer requests, poems, song lyrics, and testimonies written all over it. Pieces of paper with other notes and messages were pinned to the other walls.

I spent maybe an hour there, simply thanking God—for who He was, for His faithfulness and love, and for the people who had been saved at the show that night. I asked Him with great expectancy for the "more" I sensed would come over the next days. As I knelt and prayed, I felt as though my conversation with God was the only thing happening in the whole world.

Even now, years later, I can still feel the warmth and stillness of that small room.

After I'd prayed, I spent some time reading the short testimonies, prayers, and prophetic declarations scribbled in notebooks and chalked on the wall.

Eventually, though, I padded quietly back into the lounge, gently closing the prayer room door behind me. I tiptoed over the snoring bodies of my bandmates sprawled out across the floor to find my sleeping bag. Then I crawled inside and sank into sleep with a full heart, expectant and excited about what wonderful things might be waiting for me on my great adventure with God.

What my wandering mind never could have imagined was that before morning I would come face-to-face with a reality of God's nature that I had never known before.

FACEDOWN IN TERROR

I was pulled violently from sleep at about 3:00 a.m., jerked awake by screaming. With my heart pounding in my chest, I opened my eyes wide but could see nothing through the darkness. Beneath the cries, I could hear what sounded like a hammer striking a board over and over again.

I balled my fists tightly around the soft fabric of my sleeping bag as I listened intently, trying to make sense of exactly what was going on. As the fog of sleep lifted off me, I realized what was happening.

There was a woman on the "night watch" in the adjoining prayer room, and she had turned on music and was worshiping God loudly and crying out for Him to move in her family and her church. Alone in the early hours, probably unaware—and if not, certainly unconcerned—that five guys were sleeping nearby, she stood shouting, clapping, and weeping in the holy presence of God.

"Yahweh!" she shouted. "You are holy! You are worthy! Send Your Spirit and heal our land!" Pouring her heart and soul into every word, she cried with such passion and desperation that her voice began to crack, but she persisted. "Send Your Spirit and heal our land! Send Your Spirit and heal our land! Holy One! Holy One!"

The other guys had stirred and muttered something, half-awake, when she'd first crashed into our consciousness, but then turned over and burrowed back down into sleep.

But I was wide awake, rooted in place. I could not have moved if I had wanted to. As I sensed the prayer warrior's appeals touching the heart of heaven over and over again, I could feel waves of what I can only describe as God's glory begin to wash over me.

Sometimes, when you stand on a stage as the sound techs check the subwoofers, it feels as if the sound is flowing up into your body from the ground, making every cell vibrate. This was what I was experiencing, though even more intensely. It wasn't just sound; it was spirit too—something so all-encompassing, so intense that I felt I might somehow melt into the floor. This was God in a way I had never known before.

Now that I had some sense of what was happening, the fear that had first gripped me when I jolted awake didn't subside—rather, it intensified. As I listened to this unseen woman's pursuit of God and His presence, the holiness and weight of the moment bore down upon me. I felt unworthy to experience it.

I had prayed before, but I'd never prayed like that. I had known significant experiences with God, led hundreds to Christ, and seen some astonishing miracles, but I had never experienced anything like what I felt in those moments. For the first time in my life, I had been touched by real terror—*holy fear.*

One thought haunted me as it replayed in my mind over the next hour: *God is in the room.* Not that "presence of God" so often casually talked about in church, or the theological idea that an omnipresent God is always everywhere. I mean, the tangible weight and glory of Yahweh Elohim—the One Elijah called "the God who answers by fire" (1 Kings 18:24)—had filled the room and pinned me to the floor.

I lay there on the brown carpet, drenched in sweat, trembling, while tears rolled down my cheeks. This was *holy.* There was a power and gravity in the room beyond anything I could ever hope to fully describe.

I was unnerved, overwhelmed, undone. While I knew the presence was holy, its utter purity was beyond anything I had ever even imagined—brighter than the brightest light, hotter than the hottest flame. It felt as though it might be too much for me to bear.

It was like one of those moments in an action movie when the hero runs for cover as something explodes into a giant ball of flame behind him. Then he ducks behind a wall or slips into a doorway as the sheet of flame roars over and past him, consuming everything in its path. All he can do is keep down, stay still, and hold his breath.

Perhaps that was what Moses felt like when God's presence passed behind him as he hid in the cleft of the rock (Exodus 33).

All I knew was that I could not speak or stand. Only by keeping still and lying facedown did I feel I might be safe; I feared that if I moved, I may die. This was not a presence that coddles or excites; it was a presence that rips, ravages, and burns. I felt, not wonder or awe, but plain *fear*.

I didn't know why God had let me experience this. I was unworthy, but He had allowed it anyway. Unconcerned about my capacity to endure or process it, He'd simply come in His glory and left me ruined on the floor.

Despite my familiarity with the stories and concepts of Scripture, the sheer intensity of His holiness was more than I could have possibly imagined or anticipated. I lay unmoving, confronted by the fearful truth that though I thought I had known a lot about God, actually I was still only at the beginning—of the beginning.

Somewhere before dawn I finally fell into an exhausted sleep. When I woke again, it was quiet. As we broke camp and readied to head out on the road, some of the other guys grumbled about how that wild woman had woken them up in the middle of the night with all her noise.

I kept quiet. I felt too raw, too stunned, too vulnerable to speak, as if in doing so I might somehow trivialize or taint what had happened. It was too pure, too powerful, too precious, too everything to begin to try to put into words. So I kept it all to myself.

I never saw the woman who had worshiped so loudly on the other side of the wall, never learned her name, but her pursuit of God had opened a door for me to encounter Him as I never had before. I didn't understand all that had happened, but I sensed I would never be the same again.

That night in the trailer marked me. It haunted my thoughts in the weeks and months that followed, always hanging in the back of my mind as I sat through happy, casual worship services. I wondered often about the power, the weight, and the glory that had pressed down on me as I lay next to that little prayer room. I listened to many great messages in many great churches, but I never really heard God described the way I had encountered Him back there.

I have had some similar moments since then, though they are not common. Powerful as those occasions have been, I have not sought them out just for the sake of having them. I have been more interested in what it means to express the reality of those experiences and in how I should live differently as a result of this greater sense of the fear of the Lord.

Over the next few years, as I continued to grow in my walk with Him, I began to gain some understanding. I discovered that this fierce, wild, weighty presence I'd met in that mobile home was not merely a profoundly personal experience; it was also a deeply biblical one.

As I studied Scripture, the Spirit of God showed me that fear was not only something God evoked in me; it was something He demanded of me. I learned that God attaches the condition of holy fear to blessing, mercy, long life, protection, glory, and even power.

There are promises made specifically—sometimes exclusively—to those who "fear the Lord." And He relates in a different way to those who fear Him than He does to those who simply believe, those who pray, or even those who love Him.

I came to realize that God had not come to scare me to death, that night in the trailer. Rather, He had come to scare me to life—the life spoken of in John 17:3: "This is eternal life, that they might know You, the only true God, and Jesus Christ whom You have sent." It's the abundant, wild life Jesus died for me to have.

How can something that seems so negative—sheer terror—ever result in something so positive—everlasting life? Fair question. The answer requires an openness to being stretched and challenged, and a willingness to look at some familiar Bible passages from unfamiliar perspectives and give God permission to blow away the cobwebs of dead religion that may be obscuring your view of who He really is. Because if we cannot see Him as He really is, we cannot know Him as He really is; and if we cannot really know Him, we will inevitably settle for less than the life He intended for us.

SAFE FROM THE FIRESTORM

One night, in the midst of a long season of study and intense prayer while preparing to write this book, the Lord gave me a dream that left me shaken deeply and astonished at His power. When I awoke, I did so with a clearer understanding of the "scary" nature of God and a firmer grasp of the beauty of my position in Him than I'd ever had before.

In the dream, I was standing in wide-open land with my family. The horizon seemed to stretch away forever all around us. I knew this vast area had been given to me, to us. It was ours to live in, to live from, to live off of. We should have been overjoyed, but instead we were overwhelmed.

That's because the whole area looked as though the life had been choked out of it. Where there should have been acres of crops, there was instead an endless lattice of thick, thorny vines. They ran over the ground like tangled, brittle Christmas lights. In the gaps between them, weeds poked up from the dry, thirsty ground. The rocky earth was dusty and lifeless. It was expansive, but it was useless.

It all seemed hopeless. What to do? Where to start? Even with a fleet of heavy equipment, it would take forever to clear this land so we could begin to sow and tend and harvest. But I had nothing—not even a pair of gloves to put on to start pecking away at the mess by hand. We were standing in the middle of a lost cause.

I became aware of a faint tremor under my feet. It grew in intensity, and the earth began to hum and then vibrate and then shake violently. It felt like standing on a railway line with a freight train roaring toward me, the shaking running up through my entire body.

Looking up to the east, I saw a wall of thick, black smoke moving quickly toward me. It stretched from the ground way up into the sky, with flashes of a fierce orange-red occasionally coming through the black shroud.

As the wall of smoke surged closer, I could see in its midst a burning cyclone of fire. Spinning and rotating, it was as wide as a city block and higher into the sky than my eyes could see—and it was coming directly at us. We were going to die.

I grabbed my wife, Candice, and our kids by the hands, and we turned and fled from the otherworldly force that was coming for us. The earth was shaking harder beneath us, and the dark clouds hung heavy and swirled around us as we ran for a nearby storm shelter, the intensity and heat of the pillar of fire bearing down on us from behind.

We reached the shelter just in time. I flung open the doors and helped everyone down into the underground bunker, pulling the doors closed behind me not a moment too soon. The old wooden shelter creaked and rattled and threatened to break apart as the roaring tornado of fire ripped across the ground above us. We hugged one another excitedly, scarcely believing we had escaped.

But there was more. As soon as I closed the white shelter doors behind us, the emotional atmosphere of the dream shifted dramatically. The horror we'd felt while running for our lives was replaced immediately by elation. We began to celebrate the firestorm that we'd just run from, because we knew what it was doing to our dry land.

As the fire raged across the earth above us, the vines and weeds that had kept the land lifeless were being burned away. And soon, what had been an insurmountable challenge was now a tremendous opportunity—endless fields of fertile soil, ready to be worked to meet our needs. What we never could have done for ourselves had been achieved on our behalf by an all-consuming fire. The thing we had feared might kill us had, in fact, made new life possible.

My experience in pursuit of the fear of the Lord has been a lot like that dream. Yahweh's utter holiness is a relentless and intensely unstoppable force, and it will completely consume anything left outside of the shelter of my dream—a shelter I now know as "Christ." There is only one place that our lives are safe from the consuming fire of God's holy presence, and that is the place of abiding. Seated and hidden in Christ.

Now, when my family and I stepped into Christ, our shelter, the spinning, raging pillar of fire above didn't suddenly turn into a butterfly farm. It was still just as violent and forceful as it was before. It wasn't the fire that changed; what changed was my position in relation to the fire.

THERE IS ONLY ONE PLACE THAT OUR LIVES ARE SAFE FROM THE CONSUMING FIRE OF GOD'S HOLY PRESENCE, AND THAT IS THE PLACE OF ABIDING.

I have lived most of my life in a church culture that has tried to teach us that our God is passive, weak, and indifferent. We have developed theologies and philosophies that offer excuses for the seeming absence of His power or presence with us, and we have diminished the indescribable glory of His weighty nearness to a short list of palatable buzzwords like *uplifting* or *family-friendly* or *safe*.

But don't we need a God who is more than that? When your marriage is hanging on by a thread, don't you need a God who is more than just "safe"? When your kids' faith is being shaken by the seductive song of a godless culture, and the call of secular humanism is growing louder in their ears, don't you need a God who is more than an "uplifting" idea?

As true, biblical faith finds itself on the chopping block of inclusivity and religious relevance, we more than ever need a God who is not subject to our ever-shifting philosophies or worldviews. One who is not open for debate but One who cannot—will not—be tamed for the comfort of a self-indulgent generation.

In my divine dream, I had seen a massive, devouring cyclone of fire. And when forced to face my own severe inadequacy amid the thorny ground, that devouring fire was my only hope.

Whether the thorns choking the life from the soil of your heart are thorns of pride, addiction, depression, doubt, hatred, rejection, or deception, you will find, as I did, that if you will hide yourself in the shelter called Christ, the holy fire of God's presence will burn those thorns away, creating a tenderness and a fruitfulness that you could never have established on your own.

Let's Pray

Yahweh,

I long to be left awestruck and undone by the fire of Your glory.

I ask You now to visit me with Your intensity and holiness, and ruin me for casual Christianity.

Show me who You truly are, so I might worship You like You truly deserve, amen.

CHAPTER 2

THE TWO SIDES OF FEAR

Now therefore, let the fear of the Lord be upon you.
—2 Chronicles 19:7

I hadn't been with For Today long when a friend asked me a question that threw me for a loop.

We used to stay at Bitsy's house when we played shows in her area in Minnesota—her parents let us crash in their basement. She and I were out driving one day, just running errands and talking about our lives and what we thought God had for us in the future, when I confessed to her that while I was so honored to be able to tour the world, playing our music and sharing Jesus with so many lost and hurting young people, I felt that it was merely my job, and that I hadn't yet discovered my true purpose.

Then she asked me a seemingly unrelated question: "Mattie, what do you think is the biggest problem in the world?"

I scrambled to come up with a good answer. Selfishness, maybe. Or inequality, perhaps. How about global warming? Suicide? Extremism, racism, sexism, or some other "ism." So many weighty possibilities came to mind.

But then it came from somewhere deep inside, welling up, my real answer.

"Fear, Bitsy," I found myself saying. "I think the biggest problem in the world is fear."

She looked at me. "Well then, Mattie, you should spend your life fixing that problem."

I didn't realize it at the time, but now I believe that was the first time I felt I had a real assignment from God.

As I began to think about it more in the days that followed, it became clearer to me that in my unexpected response, I had hit on something.

All the other answers I could have given would have been right to a point but would not have been universal. Each possibility, however, shared a common denominator with all the others. *Fear.*

I sometimes saw the fear in the faces of some of our fans. I loved the passion and life they brought to our shows, but there were occasions when I'd see something beneath the energy: fear. They covered it over with anger or they feigned indifference. Some of them lived indulgent, self-destructive lives, while others adopted a mantra of militant self-preservation. Underneath it all, though, was fear of being rejected, fear of there being no place for them, fear of being alone.

In the metal music scene, many of the fans found some kindred spirits and a way to express some of their pain, but they couldn't outrun the fear. While they presented an angry, hardened image to the world, inside they were just scared kids. Depression, addiction, and suicide were rampant in that subculture.

They weren't unique in this either. As my worldview has grown and expanded, I have seen that this driving force called fear manifests itself in every other culture as well, just in different ways. Instead of rebellion, many allow fear to drive them to conformity. They go along to get along, making sure they don't rock the boat.

Fear drives some people to stand up and try to break out and others to sit down and try to fit in. Fear can make you either uptight or uninterested. You sweat over every exam, determined to get an A, or you skate through school half-heartedly because you don't want to risk failure. Different manifestations, same fear.

Fear can be concrete and abstract. Some of the most common flesh-and-blood fears are fear of the dark, fear of flying, fear of spiders, fear of heights, and fear of public speaking. When it comes to the emotional realm, some common fears are fear of commitment, fear of failure, fear of intimacy, fear of inadequacy, and fear of rejection.

Fear can cause you to hold on tight or to let go. When some people lose someone they love, they get overprotective about those they still have. They become obsessive about eating well and having the best possible insurance policy and only buying cars with all the latest safety features.

After my dad died the winter after my eighth birthday, I went the other way. I decided that it would be easier to say goodbye if I never got too attached to anyone. You'll never lose someone you need if you never need anybody, was my reasoning.

I never noticed that I'd made that fearful adjustment until ten years later, when I graduated from high school. At our graduation ceremony, all my friends were crying and hugging on each other, reminiscing about the good times we'd had and talking about how badly they'd miss each other. I, on the other hand, was wondering how long it would take to get it all over with so I could get to Taco Bell for lunch. (This is an area in which I'm still learning.) Out of fear, I had disengaged from my friends—that way I could never be hurt.

Fear is big business. Of course, not all clinical anxiety or depression can be blamed on fear, but it's certainly a significant factor—and one in six Americans has taken some kind of antidepressant or sedative to deal with these diagnoses.[1] Then there's all the money we spend to be prepared in case bad things happen. The average American gives around a tenth of their overall income to health insurance coverage and deductibles.[2]

A RISK-TAKING WORLD

While on the one hand, we humans do everything we can to stifle fear, we also have this unexplainable, subconscious longing to experience it. Just look at the growth of extreme sports over the past couple of decades—people pushing themselves to the limits of their physical capabilities and endurance.

This may be a small group of on-the-edgers, but the rest of us like to watch them, even if it's through splayed fingers covering our faces. I remember being a kid, watching daredevil biker Evel Knievel's daredevil biker son Robbie jump his motorcycle across the Grand Canyon. I cringed the whole time, but I couldn't look away. Other than music videos, some of the most-watched clips on social media are of people doing crazy things, like walking around without a security harness on top of high buildings.

Even people who would never consider doing something like that themselves seek a brush with fear, though a safer one. Theme parks spend millions of dollars to create rides and experiences that give people a rush without too much risk. Then there are scary movies: 2017 was the biggest year ever for horror movies in the United States. They brought in almost $1 billion at the box office.[3] What's *that* all about?

There's something about fear that seems to somehow drive many of us away and yet draw us in simultaneously. It's not uncommon to hear someone say, after surviving some death-defying experience, that he never felt more alive, more of a rush, than when he was so close

to death. Studies have shown that people feel stronger and more confident after having watched a scary movie, or ridden a roller coaster,
because they faced and overcame their fear.

I wonder whether Moses said that very thing after he came
away from his encounter with God on a smoke-shrouded, thunder-
ing mountain (Exodus 19). Isaiah may have done the same after his
encounter with God in a smoke-filled temple (Isaiah 6). And John
may have echoed their sentiments after an encounter with God on the
island of Patmos that left him prostrate.

I believe that the push-pull, love-hate sort of relationship so many of
us have with fear is a sign of our unique humanity. It's one of the finger-
prints of God on the human soul, a sign of our hunger for something
shocking and unexplainable, something that is bigger than we are.

Dr. Mark Eckel, president of the Comenius Institute at Indiana
University–Purdue University Indianapolis (IUPUI), would agree.
Having taught high school classes on Gothic
horror novels such as *Dracula* and *The
Strange Case of Dr. Jekyll and Mr. Hyde*, he
has also studied horror movies for years and
believes that the horror genre is "the closest to
the Christian view of life." Why? Because it
"acknowledges the supernatural, evil, hopes
for salvation," he says, "and asks the ques-
tion, 'Is there someone to whom I must give an account?'"[4] According
to Eckel, we often substitute cheap thrills and chills for the true fear of
God because "we can't live with God and we can't live without Him."[5]

> THE PUSH-PULL,
> LOVE-HATE SORT OF
> RELATIONSHIP SO
> MANY OF US HAVE WITH
> FEAR IS A SIGN OF OUR
> UNIQUE HUMANITY.

A TIMID CHURCH

This widespread fear has presented a tremendous opportunity to the
church. As A. W. Tozer, one of my favorite Christian writers, once

said, "A scared world needs a fearless church."[8] If we can find a way out of the stifling fear that has infiltrated our postmodern church culture, we can become the beacon that we were always intended to be to a seeking world.

But sadly, there's a lot of fear in the church too. We may quote 1 John 4:18—how "perfect love casts out fear"—but we live our own lives just as scared, intimidated, and unsure as the world we're supposed to be transforming! Rather than stand out, as we are supposed to, like lights shining in "the midst of a crooked and perverse generation" (Phil. 2:15), we allow the fear of man to drive us to pervert and concede the very kingdom message that saved us, just so we can "fit in" with the world.

As children of an endlessly creative, inventive God, we should be the greatest innovators, but we are often lagging behind, mimicking what the world has done rather than reflecting what heaven is doing. We've stayed away from new things for fear of failure, fear of being criticized, fear of being misunderstood. This trap has robbed destiny from countless saints in these past few generations, even though God warned us of it in His Word: "The fear of man brings a snare" (Prov. 29:25).

The apostle John declared that "He who is in you is greater than he who is in the world" (1 John 4:4), but we have unwittingly reversed that. We hide in the safety of our churches and work endlessly to develop a culture of comfort, scared that if we go outside we might somehow get infected by the dirt of the world God loves so much.

We have created a Disneyland version of the house of God, offering a safely packaged water ride that may get us a little wet, but nothing more, rather than launching out on a real, wild river where we risk finding ourselves in over our heads, being carried to a place beyond our own control.

Fear wears a lot of different masks. Sometimes it's an angry, in-your-face one, where people go on the offensive against anyone and anything because they're frightened on the inside, and they figure that the best way to keep themselves safe is to intimidate anything that threatens their way of life.

But more commonly in the modern church, fear likes to dress itself up as wisdom.

Early in my evangelistic ministry, some older Christians took me off to the side to give me some advice. While patronizingly applauding my passion for Christ and His gospel, they suggested I tone it down a little.

Oh, they, too, had once had the same zeal I had, they assured me, but as they'd gotten older and "wiser," they'd learned that we don't have to do all that stuff. In their "wisdom," they explained that they'd come to realize that everybody has their own worldview, and some people won't agree with mine, and that it's best to let people believe how they want to believe, and just be a nice guy. "That's what Jesus would do," they concluded.

Needless to say, I respectfully ignored them and the "wisdom" they were touting. The invitation of Christ has always been to a reckless, wild, unrelenting pursuit, and while that type of philosophy is foreign and often even offensive to a comfort-seeking world, it is exactly what our Jesus demands from all who would claim to follow Him.

For the last couple of generations, the big lie that the church has bought into is what we call the "prosperity gospel," the idea that God's primary purpose for His followers is for them to be wealthy and comfortable, and if we will just pray the right prayers in the right way, He will have to cough up blessings, like a divine ATM. The prosperity gospel teaches that the evidence of God's hand on a person or a ministry is the financial wealth with which they've been entrusted.

Now, don't misunderstand me. I love God's blessings. But I am also very aware that whether His abundant provision to me is financial or spiritual, my calling is to steward that abundance, not hoard it.

God wants to use me as the means by which He blesses the world, not use the world as the means by which He blesses me.

If the prosperity gospel was the major deception in parts of the church of my parents' generation, then the major deception in mine is, as a friend of mine calls it, the "popularity gospel." Many seem to so desperately long to seem relevant, cool, and hip that they will do almost anything to be accepted by the world.

We are apparently so unconvinced of the worthiness of Jesus that we beseech our friends to come to church with us for the coffee and donuts, or the great worship band, or the amazing new building, or the pizza party outreach event. We have a million things to offer—with the presence of a holy God in the fine print near the bottom, if there at all.

The subtle danger in all this is that we settle for the idea that the church should just be "nice." We end up believing that being godly means being nonconfrontational. God's people are no longer "bold as a lion" (Prov. 28:1); instead, we're nonthreatening yes-people who have been duped by the spirit of religion into thinking that we can flatter people into the kingdom.

I have seen how fear can even be at work in the lives of Christians who aren't passive or indifferent, who want to be part of changing the world with God. I know people who have enjoyed God's favor, have experienced His blessings, and are walking in a special measure of His glory, but privately they admit to wondering when the other shoe is going to drop.

A troubling fear in the back of their minds tells them, *It can't go on like this forever. It's got to come crashing down at some stage. All good things come to an end.* They are well aware that God is working in them significantly, but they are plagued by a fear that He's going to suddenly pull the rug out from under them as a surprise "character-building" exercise.

No! Where do we see that in the Bible? Is that really the promise of God, that things will be okay for a while, but then they'll inevitably start to go wrong?

That's not what I find. I read of a God who is establishing a kingdom of perpetual increase, in which I constantly get to experience more—more joy, more peace, more of Him.

I read that "of the increase of His government and peace there will be no end" (Isa. 9:7) and that we His children are being transformed "from glory to glory" (2 Cor. 3:18). That sounds like progress, not setback, to me! That is not a roller-coaster ride; it's an eternal ascension.

When it comes down to it, most fear is of the unknown. It's about uncertainty, of not being in control. That is what keeps so many of us from stepping out and trusting God. We aren't sure He is going to come through. If we're honest, we believe in God, but we don't really believe God.

I'm reminded of the example of the African gazelle. It is actually remarkably agile, capable of springing up to thirty feet and jumping quite high. Yet it can be corralled by a small fence standing no more than three feet tall. Why? Because if it can't see what's on the other side, where it is going to land, it won't jump.

What about you? Have you allowed your fears to tame you? Are you content to stay in your cage, as it were, where you're fed and cared for, or will you choose to jump into the wild unknown, where freedom and boundless discovery await?

WHEN FEAR IS A GOOD THING

What does Tozer's fearless church look like? At the end of the day, does it really mean it has no fear? Actually, fear can be a good thing. It can keep us from putting ourselves in dangerous situations. While I do love the adrenaline rush of a tall roller coaster, or even standing up to preach the gospel in the middle of a crowded restaurant, it is ultimately a healthy fear that strengthens my judgment and keeps me from taking unnecessarily dangerous risks.

Healthy fear can also keep unhealthy curiosity in check. Our desire to explore, to learn new things, to investigate is part of the way God designed us. Our inquisitive human nature has led to countless innovations and discoveries that have enriched our lives in innumerable ways, but there is potentially a dark side to our inherent curiosity too. As a parent, I've had to say, "Don't touch!" or "Don't eat that!" to my boys on more occasions than I can possibly remember. My sons' desire to experience the world around them, while a beautiful thing, can also be dangerous if not guided and protected properly.

Like a loaded gun, curiosity needs to be handled properly. It needs to be shepherded and stewarded. We all know what curiosity did to the cat, and it's gotten people into all sorts of other difficulties too.

The Enemy would love to use our curiosity to take us places we don't need to go.

I wonder what I'll find if I click on this link.

I wonder if that attractive person from accounting will be at the office lunch.

I wonder what those pick-me-up pills are like.

I wonder whether this cable series is as racy as people say.

Healthy fear can keep us out of harm's way. And not only can it protect us from harm, but it can also drive us to growth.

After the encounter with Dad and Brock that I shared in the introduction, I never got bullied again. But while I may not usually be intimidated by people, my sweet, petite, one-hundred-pound wife did make my knees shake one day. It was when she told me she was pregnant for the first time. I had to hold on to a chair to steady myself, for fear of falling over.

Yes, I was excited and delighted, but that wasn't what made me wobble. It was because I was scared. I thought about how young we were, how we didn't have a house or a stable income. I felt so unprepared, so unqualified to be responsible for a new life. The gravity of it all pressed down on me.

Those healthy fears awoke in me a desire and a determination to do all that I could to be ready for when our baby was born. They continue to motivate me to do all that I can to be the very best father I can for my boys.

That's something of what the fear of the Lord is about. It keeps us from making poor choices that can have negative consequences. God doesn't hate sin because He's a killjoy. Actually, He hates sin because He knows it kills joy.

As Spurgeon knew, when he compared the fear of God to a lion, if we have a true, holy fear of Yahweh and all He is, then all our other fears will melt away. We won't care what others think or say because we will only be concerned about pleasing the One whose opinion really matters.

At one For Today show, a fan told me that he loved our music and how I was not afraid to share the gospel in any situation. I had to put him right.

"Man, I've got to be honest," I told him. "I don't preach the way I do because I'm not afraid of what will happen if I preach the gospel. I preach the way I do because I am more afraid of what might happen if I *don't* preach the gospel."

I went on to tell him that I preached the gospel so relentlessly because I had come to know how fierce and serious and severe God is, and because I knew the severity of God, His kindness was infinitely more precious to me.

Yes, on the other side of God's terror, I found God's kindness to be so much more vivid and dynamic than I'd ever known. Yet if I'd not yielded to the pruning of fear, I would have just done my best to love half of God with a heart that longed to know all of Him.

How awful it would be if no one ever told the kids at our concerts that the loving-kindness of God was matched with a severity that should spur everyone to seek His grace and mercy.

THE OPPOSITE OF FEAR

If the fear you're experiencing is not a healthy kind, then you need to deal with it. But how? Just by gritting your teeth and trying to be brave? "Getting a grip" on yourself? No, because the opposite of fear isn't courage, it's faith. It's trusting that God is good, come what may. It's stepping out and doing what God has told you to do, despite how you feel inside. To be fearless doesn't mean to never feel afraid. It means to never let that feeling take the driver's seat of your life.

I once heard a pastor say, "You can't stop a bird from landing on your head, but you don't have to let it make a nest there." Feelings may come knocking, but you can choose whether to let them move in or not. Ultimately, true courage means choosing the path of righteousness no matter what feelings you may have to walk through along the way.

Inspired by my conversation with Bitsy, which I mentioned at the opening of this chapter, several years later I wrote what would become one of For Today's most popular songs, "Fearless," which includes the following lines:

> *We will not*
> *We will not*
> *We will not*
> *Be afraid*
> *We are fearless*
> *Fearless*
> *We bear the mark of the uncreated God*
> *So what should we fear?*

We bear the scars of the Holy Risen Son
So tell me what should we fear?
Every threat is hollow
Because our victory is already set in stone
Though we stand in this dark valley
We will not be afraid
For we know that You are near
He can't stop the kingdom
You'll see him bow at the throne on Judgment Day
So let the devil come

I wish you could have been there with me, to see a thousand young people jumping all over each other as they danced and sweated and sang those words at the top of their lungs. That is the kind of fearlessness—the kind of faith—that will enable us to stand up for righteousness, for integrity, for purity, for the standards and the Word of God in the face of a world that is increasingly hostile to Him.

It may sound contradictory, but being fearless doesn't mean eliminating all fear from your life. It means eliminating the wrong kind of fear—fear that denies the truth of who our God is, that denies He is greater than anything that may come against us—which can only be replaced with the right kind of fear—fear that acknowledges the truth of who our God is. The right kind of fear is not a fear of anything in the world, but a fear of something above and beyond and before it. The fear of the Lord, like Spurgeon's mighty lion, chases away all other fears.

Because the church has been taught, "Don't be afraid" so much, we have failed to recognize that God Himself is scary. He, like the thunderous cyclone of fire from my dream, ripping its way across our land and devouring everything in its path, is a Force to be reckoned with. But we don't have to be afraid of Him, if we've found shelter—seated in a place called Christ.

Now, suddenly, the thing we had every reason to fear is doing for us, in us, around us, all the things we never could have accomplished ourselves. The impossible is becoming easy and the unimaginable is becoming common. God can truly be God in our lives if we will simply find the right place to hide, as in my firestorm dream.

Let's Pray

Father,

    I ask that You would work righteous fear in me and deliver me from unrighteous fear.

    Make me bold and courageous in my stand for You, and uphold me by the wonderful power of Your truth, amen.

CHAPTER 3

THE FRUITS OF GODLY FEAR

Now therefore, fear the LORD, serve
Him in sincerity and in truth.
—JOSHUA 24:14

W hen people ask me how living in the fear of the Lord has made a difference in my life, one of the stories that immediately comes to mind is about Fire Wolf.

That's how he introduced himself to me after a particularly tense For Today show in Cleveland, Ohio, in the winter of 2009.

For the uninitiated, hardcore shows aren't your typical well-behaved music events. People don't sit and listen politely or hold up their cell phones to light their favorite songs. They become part of the show, throwing themselves into the music—and each other. With hundreds of amped-up kids crammed into a small venue, and the music pounding and lights flashing and spinning, things can get intense.

I was used to all that, but this night there was an ugly edge to all the energy. It came from a pretty small kid I spotted to the rear of the mosh pit in front of the stage. He was probably only about 120 pounds, a wisp of a thing, but he kept sneaking up behind people as they were getting into the music and sucker-punching them in the face before ducking away back into the crowd. It had nothing to do with enjoying music; he was simply trying to hurt people.

Then he clocked one guy who turned around and angrily pushed back, prompting a bunch of the sneaky kid's friends to pile in on the victim. I could see that the young man who had reacted to being punched was going to get hurt if someone didn't do something quickly. I decided to speak up.

Halting the music, I called out the troublemaker in front of everyone. I told him that I'd seen what he was doing. I told him that he was acting like a coward, and that stuff was never welcome at our shows. He and his buddies hated it. They were embarrassed and angry. They screamed and spat at me, making all kinds of threats as we resumed our set.

Throughout all this, I'd noticed a man standing close to the front of the stage. He was a goateed black guy, wearing a leather jacket with spiked shoulders over a sweatshirt that had flames of fire printed all along the hood. On his head was a ball cap with a wolf embroidered on the front. While everyone else was jumping and bouncing all around him, he just stood with his arms crossed, looking up at me.

When the set finished, it was time for the band to make our way to the merch table, where we'd get to meet with fans. I always looked forward to this, hoping there'd be an opportunity to tell someone about Jesus. But this time I was a little apprehensive, knowing I would have to make my way past the group I'd confronted. While I could take care of myself, I didn't like to need to.

As I got down from the stage, the guy with the ball cap moved in close and headed the same direction as me, to the back of the room. I sort of held my breath as I passed the group of troublemakers, but they seemed not to even notice me, as if there were some kind of invisible barrier between us. In fact, of the ten or so young guys in that group, not one of them so much as glanced in my direction. I walked right through their conversation, and they continued talking as if I didn't even exist.

When I arrived at the merch table, I spent some time chatting with fans, aware that the guy in the leather jacket was standing off to one side, his arms still folded, just watching. It was as if he were working security for us.

Eventually I broke away and went over to him to say hi. I asked him his name.

"I'm Fire Wolf," he said. "Sorry about those guys . . . but you all put on a great show tonight."

I thanked him and asked if he was familiar with our music.

"Oh yeah," he told me. "Everyone where I'm from listens to you."

And he turned to head out of the building.

Suddenly I had a strong sense that he hadn't been talking about his neighborhood in Cleveland. I was abruptly reminded of Hebrews 13:2, which tells of some who have "unwittingly entertained angels." And I wanted to entertain this one.

Wittingly.

So I followed Fire Wolf outside of the venue until it was just the two of us, standing alone on the street. It was much quieter out there, and I shouted, "Hey, Fire Wolf! Wait up!" He stopped and turned around.

As I drew closer to him, I pulled my wallet out of my back pocket. I don't really know what I expected an angel to do with the sixty dollars I handed him (it was all the money I had to my name), but I gave it anyway. I knew enough about the kingdom to know that you always give back to God's means of provision for you—whether that means is a pastor, a spiritual leader, a guest speaker at your church, or an angel. So I went with that. Honor is always a good strategy.

He reached out and took the money from my hand, sliding it down into the pocket of his black leather jacket. He didn't protest or ask why I was giving it to him. He knew.

He spent the next ten to fifteen minutes teaching me about the throne room of God and singing a song he'd written there; then Fire Wolf said goodbye and disappeared into the cold Cleveland night.

So, what does that strange encounter have to do with the fear of the Lord? Well, as I've said, I believe that God has attached the condition of fear to several of His biblical promises.

There are promises made specifically and sometimes even exclusively to those who fear Him. My encounter with Fire Wolf illustrates one of eight treasures I have found while exploring the character of God through the lens of holy fear: protection, perspective, presence, provision, promotion, pleasure, power, and purity.

PROTECTION: KNOWING GOD'S SAFEKEEPING

I believe that Fire Wolf's appearance that night in Cleveland was an outworking of the promise found in Psalm 34:7: "The angel of the LORD encamps around those who fear Him, and rescues them" (NASB). Notice that it doesn't say God will dispatch help when it's needed. It says that the angel of the Lord is encamped around you—on permanent deployment.

Though I never saw Fire Wolf again, the band never needed divine protection more than we did that night. Looking back, one of the most beautiful parts of that night in Cleveland was that Fire Wolf was there well before there was any tension or violence. He had been dispatched on my behalf well before I ever even knew to pray for protection.

There is no scheme of the Enemy that has ever taken God by surprise, and He has already implemented a wonderful plan to protect, prosper, and promote His children in the earth!

Look at what happened for those who feared God in Malachi:

> Then those who feared the LORD spoke to one another, and the LORD listened and heard them; so a book of remembrance was written before Him for those who fear the Lord and who meditate on His name. "They shall be Mine," says the LORD of hosts, "on the day that I make them My jewels. And I will spare them as a man spares his own son who serves him." (3:16–17)

This promise of divine protection for those who fear God is echoed in Proverbs 19:23: "The fear of the LORD leads to life, and he who has it will abide in satisfaction; he will not be visited with evil." Proverbs 14:27 says, "The fear of the LORD is a fountain of life, to turn one away from the snares of death." In 2 Kings 17:39, we read, "But the LORD your God you shall fear; and He will deliver you from the hand of all your enemies."

Wouldn't you like to know that there's a round-the-clock, divine security detail on duty for you and your family? In Deuteronomy 5:29, God lamented, "Oh, that [My people] had such a heart in them that they would fear Me and always keep all My commandments, that it might be well with them and with their children forever!"

This promise of blessings on those who follow in your line is echoed in Luke 1:50 when in her song of praise, Mary declared, "His mercy is on those who fear Him from generation to generation."

Countless saints have seen their families devastated and their children tragically lost to the wiles of the world, but God has better for us! We can stand on these biblical promises. If we will pour ourselves into embracing the fear of the Lord, He will pour Himself into defending and sustaining our families.

Psalm 115:11 says, "You who fear the LORD, trust in the LORD; He is their help and their shield," while Proverbs 10:27 states, "The fear of the LORD prolongs days."

Having this assurance of protection has certainly been a source of comfort and strength to me. I believe that when we as a church truly experience this reality, we will be able to walk in greater boldness and confidence than ever before, in the assurance of God's sufficiency. Solomon wrote, "It will be well with those who fear God, who fear before Him" (Eccl. 8:12).

If we really believe this, we won't be intimidated by what we see in front of us because we know who is enthroned inside us. We will walk in the confidence of the promise of Exodus 23:27: "I will send My fear before you . . . and will make all your enemies turn their backs to you."

And we will find that, just as I experienced at that Cleveland show, the enemies who once cursed and threatened us are unable to even see us as we walk in the divine protection of God. He will "prepare a table for [us] in the presence of [our] enemies" (Ps. 23:5).

PERSPECTIVE: HEARING GOD'S SECRETS

The book of Proverbs is full of godly wisdom—so many chapters of great insight and sound counsel from Solomon, the wisest man who ever lived (1 Kings 4:30–31).

If you want advice on pretty much anything, from marriage to business, you'll find it here. But note where Solomon says it all springs from: "The fear of the LORD is the beginning of knowledge . . . [and] of wisdom" (Prov. 1:7; 9:10). He's not talking here about being widely read or studying hard. His point is *heart* knowledge, not head knowledge. It's not a matter of knowing what to do in every situation. It's a matter of knowing who to turn to for direction and counsel no matter the situation.

"Trust in the LORD with all your heart, and lean not on your own understanding," Solomon wrote, "in all your ways acknowledge Him, and He shall direct your paths" (3:5–6).

Success in life depends completely on being tuned in to God's voice so you can detect it above the noise of the world. Proverbs 1 says that "wisdom cries aloud in the street, in the markets she raises her voice; at the head of the noisy streets she cries out" (vv. 20–21 ESV). Wisdom is speaking; are you listening?

Look where walking in that kind of wisdom takes us. David wrote:

> *Who is the man that fears the LORD?*
> *Him shall He teach in the way He chooses.*
> *He himself shall dwell in prosperity,*
> *And his descendants shall inherit the earth.*
> *The secret of the LORD is with those who fear Him,*
> *and He will show them His covenant."*
>
> (Ps. 25:12–14)

I don't know about you, but I would like to become a trusted friend of God. The cry of my heart is for Him to confide in me the secret thoughts and desires of His heart. How many of us have wondered, *Why do bad things happen to good people? Why do we pray hard and sometimes we don't get what we asked for?* Well, just as we only share secrets with those we really trust, God will only share His deepest secrets with those who are recklessly intimate with Him, not those who are casually inquisitive about Him. He holds some things back for those who are closer to Him (Dan. 2:47; Matt. 13:11; Luke 8:10; 1 Cor. 4:1).

As we will discover, God has levels of intimacy, just as we humans do. When the mailman comes to my house, he's welcome onto the porch. When friends come over for a visit, I invite them into my family room or my kitchen. Family members may get to see my bedroom on a tour of the house, but only my kids and my wife get to climb into my bed.

In the same way, Yahweh reserves parts of who He is and how He feels for those He trusts most—those who know to fear Him. According to my friend John Bevere, "an intimate relationship and friendship with God will not even begin until the fear of God is firmly planted in our hearts."[1]

PRESENCE: MANIFESTING GOD'S KINGDOM

When we talk about revival these days, it's usually something that happens inside a church. But that cannot truly be the case. If real revival begins in the church, it will inevitably spill over into the streets. If it can be contained in your services, what you're experiencing isn't revival, it's religious enthusiasm and fanatical emotion. Heaven never sends manageable amounts of revival. Either revival is overwhelming, all-consuming, and uncontainable, or it is a man-made counterfeit and destined to fail.

YAHWEH RESERVES PARTS OF WHO HE IS AND HOW HE FEELS FOR THOSE HE TRUSTS MOST—THOSE WHO KNOW TO FEAR HIM.

I've read some of the amazing accounts of what happened during the Welsh Revival of the early 1900s. The manifest presence of God's holiness descended upon their region in such a tremendous way that history tells us it reshaped the Welsh economy and shifted the course of the nation's cultural development.

Not only did some of the pubs lose their customers, as the men gave up their beer, but the mines came to a bit of a standstill as well. The pit ponies used for hauling coal trucks were so familiar with the miners using rough language to direct them that when the newly saved men cleaned up their speech, the animals didn't understand the commands being given to them. The company actually had to buy a whole new string of ponies!

All that seems a long way from today, doesn't it? But Psalm 85:9 promises, "Surely His salvation is near to those who fear Him, that glory may dwell in our land."

That's what I want to see. I don't just want to experience God in my church, or in my private prayer time. I want to see His glory dwelling in my community, in my country. I want to see God's tangible glory resting on entire communities and cities. I want God's glory to touch the prayer meeting in your house so completely that the people drinking in the bar down the street leave the building to come find someone to tell them how their souls can be saved. If glory dwells in our land, as Psalm 85 says it can, we won't have to try to persuade people to come to our carefully arranged events and ask them to "give Jesus a chance."

Instead, if we fear Him, we'll establish ourselves in a community and be conduits of His glory. God's healing and wholeness will be released. Marriages will be restored. Businesses will flourish. Test scores at schools will improve. There will be divine and unmanufactured hunger in the hearts of the lost to be saved and the captives to be delivered. It won't be our presence or protests that bring sinners to repentance. It will be the holiness of God that exposes the depth of their need.

When God's people fear Him, He can trust them to steward His presence rightly. And when He can trust us to steward His presence, He can send it in historic ways.

PROVISION: ENJOYING GOD'S BOUNTY

For me, the big problem with the prosperity gospel is that it tends to end up becoming man-centered: What can God do for *our* sake? The question we should be asking is: What can God do for *His* sake?

I'm not suggesting that embracing the fear of the Lord is a formula for making a fortune. It will never be attached to an entitled heart; it doesn't work that way. And yet, the Bible is clear that God does bless His people, and there is a special promise for those who fear Him. You can take that to the bank—literally. Proverbs 22:4 says, "The reward of humility and the fear of the LORD are riches, honor and life" (NASB).

Nor is this an isolated reference. Psalm 34:9 declares, "O fear the LORD, you His saints; for to those who fear Him there is no want" (NASB). Psalm 31:19 extols God's goodness, which the writer said is "laid up for those who fear You."

In Psalm 111:5, the writer noted, "He has given food to those who fear Him; He will ever be mindful of His covenant." A little later, in Psalm 115:13, we read, "He will bless those who fear the LORD, both small and great."

This provision can come in unexpected ways. A while back, when I was running my debit card at the grocery store, I got the strong sense from God that I should get some cash back to have available to give to someone. Because I always try to walk in the fear of the Lord, I knew I needed to do what I felt He had said. So, I got a twenty-dollar bill and stuck it in my wallet.

A few days later, I was on a road trip with a friend when we stopped to pick up a hitchhiker. She was a skinny, older, Native American lady, with dark sunglasses under long white hair. Safely loaded into the back seat with her two big suitcases, she began to tell us her story as we headed on down the road.

She was sick, she told us, really sick—dying sick. She didn't have any close family, but she was on her way to a reservation to spend her final days among her people. When we eventually stopped to drop her off, she asked if I had any money I might give her, as she didn't have any cash, she said, and she was hungry.

"You know what?" I said. "I sure do! Funny thing is, a couple of days ago, God told me to get twenty dollars out and that someone was going to need it. He knew I was going to meet you."

I shared the gospel with her and prayed for her to be healed. I don't think she really had much interest in that part, though she took the money gratefully. And then she said that, to thank me for my generosity, she wanted to write me a check. I tried my best to decline the offer, as I was pleased to have been able to help her, but she insisted.

She took a checkbook out of her bag, telling me that she'd been in the marines in Vietnam, and had some government money she didn't want them to get back when she died. As she exited the car, she gave me the check and made me swear I'd deposit it for my family.

"Promise me," she said insistently.

"Okay, yes, ma'am," I told her, tucking it into my back pocket.

A while later, I pulled out the check. It was for twenty thousand dollars. This elderly Native American woman had asked for twenty dollars—an amount God had told me two days earlier that I'd be needing to give to someone—and she gave me in return a check for a thousand times that amount! That is supernatural provision.

PROMOTION: EXPERIENCING GOD'S FAVOR

When For Today started out, we weren't that popular. The typical turnout for a show would average around twenty people, and more than a few times we'd play for just two.

It's kind of awkward when there are more people in the band than in the audience, but we always went out and gave it everything we had. My thinking was that God was there, and He always deserved our best. We told ourselves we were really playing for an audience of One.

Over time the numbers grew. It wasn't because of slick marketing. Yes, we got better, and we grew an army of enthusiastic fans, but I don't believe even that was why we ended up playing before crowds of a couple of thousand and hitting the main stage on the Vans Warped Tour—a prestigious platform in our music scene, where our outspoken Christian presence was unusual, to say the least.

I believe it was because we were experiencing the other fruits of Proverbs 22:4, beyond material blessing: "The reward of humility and the fear of the LORD are . . . honor and life" (NASB). We were honored with the opportunity to be an influence.

While that was rewarding, we were always aware that while talent brings influence, it is character that makes influence matter.

From the get-go, I had a real sense of responsibility for what I said and did at every show—a weightiness that only increased after that nighttime encounter in the prayer trailer.

I knew I was accountable to God. I didn't want to mishandle the opportunities or the responsibilities He had given me. In fact, I took it so seriously that I moved my family to a new city to submit to spiritual authority and to live life with people who would help me be true to my calling—more about that later.

God promises to reward those who honor Him with honor of their own. There are plenty of examples of this in the Bible. Joseph, who honored God by refusing to commit adultery, went from the pit and the prison to the palace, while Daniel, who honored God by refusing to neglect prayer, also rose unexpectedly to a position of prominence and influence in Babylon. And when Nehemiah was tasked with overseeing the restoration of Jerusalem, he gave some leadership responsibility to Hananiah because "he was a faithful man and feared God more than many" (Neh. 7:2).

So it wasn't their credentials, or who they knew, that qualified these men for such important roles. It was their character, their integrity, forged in an understanding of how great a God they served, that made a way for them.

As Bible teacher and missionary Joy Dawson has observed, "Through His love we have acceptance. Through the fear of the Lord operating in our lives, we have His favor. There is a big difference."[2]

PLEASURE: TASTING GOD'S GOODNESS

Walking in the fear of the Lord is the recipe for a good life:

> *Blessed is every one who fears the LORD,*
> *Who walks in His ways.*
>
> *When you eat the labor of your hands,*
> *You shall be happy, and it shall be well with you.*
> *Your wife shall be like a fruitful vine*
> *In the very heart of your house,*
> *Your children like olive plants*
> *All around your table.*
> *Behold, thus shall the man be blessed*
> *Who fears the LORD.*
>
> (Ps. 128:1–4)

That sounds pretty good to me! But there is more. God's love for us is the cornerstone and bedrock of the gospel. As John 3:16 reminds us, "God so loved the world that He gave His only begotten Son, that whoever believes in Him should not perish but have everlasting life."

Pretty much every Christian can quote that verse, and it's a wonderful truth. The all-powerful, all-supreme Creator of the universe knows and loves you uniquely and individually—along with all the other seven billion-plus people on the planet! It's amazing to consider. The privilege of sharing that message is one of the greatest joys of my life.

But there is even more to experience of God's heart toward us for those who properly fear Him. Isaiah 11:3 says, "His delight is in the fear of the LORD."

This prophetic passage is talking about Jesus. In the previous verse, Isaiah wrote of Jesus that "the Spirit of the LORD shall rest upon Him, the Spirit of wisdom and understanding, the Spirit of counsel and might, the Spirit of knowledge and of *the fear of the LORD*" (emphasis added).

This tells us that Jesus doesn't only love people; He actually delights in those who walk in the fear of the Lord.

How would it feel to truly know that God delights in you? I believe it would bring a whole new dimension to many people's relationship with God. And it also brings its own blessings.

David offered a sobering picture of God as avenger. When he cried out to God as he was surrounded by his enemies, this is how God answered:

> Then the earth shook and trembled; the foundations of heaven quaked and were shaken, because He was angry. Smoke went up from His nostrils, and devouring fire from His mouth; coals were kindled by it. He bowed the heavens also, and came down with darkness under His feet. He rode upon a cherub, and flew; and He was seen upon the wings of the wind. He made darkness canopies around Him, dark waters and thick clouds of the skies. From the brightness before Him coals of fire were kindled. The LORD thundered from heaven, and the Most High uttered His voice. He sent out arrows and scattered them; lightning bolts, and He vanquished them. Then the channels of the sea were seen, the foundations of

the world were uncovered, at the rebuke of the LORD, at the blast of the breath of His nostrils. (2 Sam. 22:8–16)

This is a scary God. This is a fierce God coming to the rescue of one He loves. And what motivated Him? David told us in verse 20: "He delivered me because He delighted in me."

There is a revolutionary promise here. Maybe you are bound by fear—worried about your circumstances or your relationships. Perhaps it seems that the Enemy is about to overwhelm you. What's the answer?

You need God to go to war on your behalf. Even a mighty warrior like David knew that. You need God to do what only God can. He will do that for those in whom He delights—those who fear Him. So turn your attention away from all the problems and look to God. His holy fear will drive out those other fears, as He swoops down to come to your rescue.

POWER: DEMONSTRATING GOD'S KINGDOM

The more messed-up the world becomes, the more opportunity the church has to stand out above and beyond any other source of hope and help. Many people's lives are so out of whack that a few good ideas aren't going to be enough to help them. Ten tips for a better marriage won't restore their relationships. Support groups will be unable to break their addictions. They need a miracle—the power of the living God to work in their lives.

It was this, not slick preaching and PowerPoint presentations, that caused the New Testament church to grow so dynamically. The apostle Paul said:

I, brethren, when I came to you, did not come with excellence of speech or of wisdom declaring to you the testimony of God. For I determined not to know anything among you except Jesus Christ and Him crucified. I was with you in weakness, in fear, and in much trembling. And my speech and my preaching were not with persuasive words of human wisdom, but in demonstration of the Spirit and of power, that your faith should not be in the wisdom of men but in the power of God. (1 Cor. 2:1–5)

But where did that power come from and how was it released? Acts 2:43 says that on the Day of Pentecost, after the Holy Spirit had fallen on the disciples and Peter preached to several thousand, "fear came upon every soul, and many wonders and signs were done through the apostles."

Without a proper fear of the Lord, God will not entrust us with His power. God prepares us to receive power by first pruning us in the fire of fear. It makes sense: like His friendship, God's power is not something to be treated or taken lightly. He will only place His life-altering power in hands that can be trusted to steward it appropriately, and those hands belong to people who fear Him.

PURITY: HAVING GOD'S HOLINESS

This one may have you scratching your head a little. Perhaps you can see now how through the fear of the Lord we can experience God's presence and protection, receive His provision and promotion, and know His perspective and power. But purity? That sounds more like an obligation we have to Him rather than a blessing we receive from Him. More like something we try to give than something we get.

GOD PREPARES US TO RECEIVE POWER BY FIRST PRUNING US IN THE FIRE OF FEAR.

But it is actually a gift we can receive, not something we have to earn. Moses told the people, "God has come to test you . . . that His fear may be before you, so that you may not sin" (Ex. 20:20).

We can be granted the capacity to walk in purity. We don't need to be dogged by sin. We can overcome it. We can resist it and rise above it! The ability to resist sin is tied directly to our conscious fear of the Lord.

Let's Pray

Lord God,
    I see the many blessings that come from a life lived in holy fear.

    Draw me in, Father, to the place of reckless devotion.

    Teach me to fear You, that I may walk confidently in all You've intended for me, amen.

CHAPTER 4

FEAR IS A FOUR-LETTER WORD

Who among you fears the LORD?
Who obeys the voice of His Servant?
Who walks in darkness
And has no light?
Let him trust in the name of the LORD
And rely upon his God.

—Isaiah 50:10

I'll never forget the first time I held a gun. It was cold and heavy, surprisingly heavy, in my hand. A shiver of both fear and excitement ran through me as I thought of the power at my fingertips. For an awkward fourteen-year-old unsure about so much in life, it was a heady moment.

I'd been taken to the shooting range by my uncle Ian, with whom we were staying in Kenosha, Wisconsin, for the holidays.

I was excited when he asked me if I wanted to go with him, because he was something of a hero to me. He was a bit of a wild man, having served as a missionary in Colombia for decades, in parts of the country disputed by rebels, government troops, and drug cartels. He'd told stories of people coming to his meetings with the intention to kill him while he was preaching and chasing him down jungle roads in their trucks as he ran for his life. He made a point of carrying a gun.

Uncle Ian was familiar with danger, but—or maybe because of that—he wouldn't abide any danger if it wasn't absolutely necessary. At the range, he talked me through the basic rules of gun safety, showed me how to hold and aim. It was matter-of-fact, but in his tone and manner, I heard the unspoken message that is first and foremost with all firearm safety instruction: "Mattie, this thing can kill you if you don't handle it correctly."

The same thing is true of God's presence. The same presence that healed a crippled man at the Beautiful Gate in the temple in Acts 3 killed Ananias and Sapphira just two chapters later.

I don't point that out to scare you off, but to give you a sober reality check. Many Christians talk freely about wanting more of God, but they don't always stop to think of all that means. If you want God to take you to a new place, you'll have to be willing to leave behind the customs and comforts of the old place. Just as a gun needs to be approached properly, so does the pursuit of God.

Firing a gun for the first time was an incredible rush. The noise was far louder than I'd expected, the kickback so strong I thought the gun might fly back over my shoulder. It was exhilarating. And scary.

I don't know how many times, as a typical teenager, I'd ignored Uncle Ian when he'd said something to me on other occasions, but this day, with a gun in my hand, I listened and listened hard. I feared what this weapon could do, and as a result, I wanted to be sure to do everything he told me to and nothing he told me not to. So it must be for those who desire to carry even a portion of God's holiness.

CASUALNESS LEADS TO CASUALTIES

I've fired a gun countless times since that day with my uncle, both on the range and in the woods. I have guns to protect my family, to provide for them (I like to hunt when I can) and for fun. But no matter how familiar I have become with firearms, I haven't allowed myself or anyone I know to become casual around them. Because that's when bad things can happen. In a typical year, around five hundred people die in the United States from accidental shootings,[1] many of them because they don't take the danger seriously enough.

Put another way, appropriate fear leads to appropriate respect. And if that's true for guns, it is even more true for God. As Joy Dawson says, "There is a sense in which it is spiritually healthy to be afraid of God."[2]

This makes a lot of people in the church today uncomfortable. They somehow think it makes God seem too harsh, too demanding, too unloving. They are quick to say that when the Bible mentions fear in relation to God, it really means "respect," or even "awe." The problem is, the words we use don't always convey the full or same meaning that the biblical writers intended when they wrote them.

For example, I love soccer. I love apple pie with ice cream. I love movies. I love hoodies. I love Candice. Each statement is true, but they don't all mean *love* in the same way, that's for certain.

Furthermore, there are four Greek words used in the Bible that are translated *love*, each with a different meaning. *Eros* is romantic love. *Philia* is brotherly love. *Storge* is familial love. *Agape* is godly love.

In the same way, *fear* in the Bible can sometimes refer to respect. And I believe that respecting God is a good thing, for sure. But respect has to be rooted in good soil if it is going to be fruitful and bring life. It isn't just toeing the line because you don't want to hurt God's feelings.

The fact is, however, that many times the word *fear* in the Bible does not mean "respect" or "awe." It means *fear*! It's got four letters, not six, nor three.

The word *fear* appears 456 times in the New King James Version, 352 of them in the Old Testament. The phrase "the fear of the LORD" occurs 123 times, all but four in the Old Testament.

Among the Hebrew words most often used for fear in the Old Testament is *yare'*, for which *Strong's Concordance* gives the following definition: "affright, make afraid, dreadful, put in fearful reverence, terrible act." No way around it: not respect, not awe, not wonder. Plain old fear.

This is the word used in Genesis 3:10, when Adam hid after eating from the forbidden tree and told God, "I heard Your voice in the garden, and I was afraid because I was naked; and I hid myself."

It is also the word used in Genesis 32:11, when Jacob prayed for protection from his brother, Esau, "for I fear him, lest he come and attack me and the mother with the children."

In both cases, these men were fearing for their lives.

Yare' is also the word used in Psalm 34:9, when the writer urged, "O, fear the LORD, you His saints! There is no want to those who fear Him"; and in Proverbs 9:10, which tells us, "The fear of the LORD is the beginning of wisdom."

And it's the word used in Isaiah 11:3, where the prophet said of Jesus, "His delight is in the fear of the LORD."

There are many more instances, but I think you get the point. Fear means *fear*.

"Yes, but that was the Old Testament," some people say. "Things are different now that we are under a new covenant."

Not actually. Among the Greek words used for fear in the New Testament is *phobos*, from which we get our word *phobia*. *Strong's Concordance* defines it as "fear, terror, alarm; the object or cause of fear; reverence, respect." The *New American Standard Exhaustive Concordance* defines it as "panic, flight, fear, the causing of fear or terror."

This is the word used in Matthew 14:26, when Jesus walked out on the water to the disciples as they tried to cross the Sea of Galilee in difficult conditions: "And when the disciples saw Him walking on the sea, they were troubled, saying, 'It is a ghost!' And they cried out for fear." If I saw a ghost walking across some water directly toward the boat I was sailing in, the scream I let out wouldn't be a scream of "wonder" or "awe"; it would be one of absolute terror.

Phobos is also the word used in Acts 2:43, in recounting the growth of the church after the Day of Pentecost: "Then fear came upon every soul, and many wonders and signs were done through the apostles."

Again, there are more instances, but I hope the point is clear: when we read the word *fear* in Scripture, we can't always translate it as simply respect or reverence. To do so diminishes the reality of who God is and what He promises us and requires of us.

WITHOUT APPROPRIATE FEAR, WE BECOME INAPPROPRIATELY CASUAL

How have we managed to get this "fear of the Lord" thing so wrong? Partly because to equate fear with *reverence* or *awe* is more comfortable and comforting, more convenient, I believe. It's less demanding of us.

If we truly fear Yahweh, if we understand just how fierce, fiery, magnificent, stunning, and wild He is, right respect will naturally follow. But if we simply teach people to respect a God they've not learned to fear, their respect will be inadequate, casual, and insignificant, built on a foundation of obligation, not revelation.

True righteous respect is a by-product of having been gripped with fear, so if we try to instruct people into just "respecting" God appropriately, it won't work. They may do what they are told, but their hearts won't be in the right place.

Frankly, I see that in some of the churches I get to visit. God's people are coming together to worship, honor, and hear from their great King, and yet they seem to treat it less like a royal audience and more like a trip to the mall or the movie theater.

I'm not suggesting we need a dress code for church, but some people look as though they have just rolled out of bed or, worse, that they are heading out to a nightclub later. I doubt they would turn up like that for a meeting with the president—or, if they did, that his people would let them in. A friend who was invited to a meeting with President Obama told me later that before the president came into the room, everyone was briefed on what to do and what not to do. They were expected to show due respect.

IF WE SIMPLY TEACH PEOPLE TO RESPECT A GOD THEY'VE NOT LEARNED TO FEAR, THEIR RESPECT WILL BE INADEQUATE, CASUAL, AND INSIGNIFICANT.

Is it rude or inappropriate to expect the same respect in the presence of the King? Or what about the one the King has put into our lives as a spiritual authority? Most of us would extend some level of respect to the president, who is leading the country—even if we don't like or agree with him, we acknowledge the weight of his position—but what about the person who is responsible for our souls? The pastor, who is leading God's people, steps up to preach, and we're busy texting or chatting or wondering where to go for lunch after the service.

I believe you can tell a lot about a church by the way its members treat their pastor or the guest speaker who has been invited to bring

God's Word. If we will honor the one who carries the Word, we will inevitably find that the Word they carry will have a greater effect on us.

I have been in churches where the pastor has to fight for the congregation's attention. I've also been in churches where the pastor is clearly uncomfortable, insecure, and even afraid to mention the offering to the people. That shouldn't be! If we will recognize the position God has given our spiritual leaders in our lives, we should be grateful for the opportunity to hear from, or give to, them.

We get to be part of God's family on earth, the church. The common lack of regard for that privilege also reveals a lack of appropriate reverence for the order God has established in the world, which in turn points to a failure to give Him the honor He is due. We claim to trust God, but then we accuse Him when we accuse those He placed in authority of being unfit for the positions He gave them.

There are a number of factors behind this modern church trend, to be sure. But the most common is that we've built our churches to function more like corporations than like families. This denies God's design in exchange for the design taught to us by Babylon— the system of the world.

In many churches the pastor is more of a CEO than a spiritual authority, accountable to the "shareholders" rather than to God. As a result, people become consumers rather than co-laborers. They shop around for what suits them, and if the preacher says something they don't like, they simply move on to another church down the street.

But God intended church to be family. You don't get to fire family members when you have problems with them. You don't get to give up on family. You stick it out and you work it out because you are bound by blood—just as, in the church, we are made into one body by the blood of Christ.

Then there is the way respect has been devalued in the wider culture. A hundred years ago—even thirty—society had a much greater sense of the need for respect. These days, everyone still wants to be respected: people are quick to take offense if someone says something they don't like. They don't want to be "dissed," but neither do they want to give respect to others. "Respect has to be earned," they say.

Actually, no. Soldiers don't wait until they feel their officers have "proved themselves" before following orders. Not if they want to avoid a dishonorable discharge. An employee doesn't get to decide what he thinks of his boss before doing what he was hired to do. Not if he wants to keep getting a paycheck.

Once, when my pastor announced a work day at our church, he didn't tell everyone they had to be there, but we knew that it was important to him. It wasn't a requirement; it was an opportunity for us to show him honor. Early the next Saturday morning, *every single man in the entire church* was there, ready to go—and with all of us pulling our weight, we finished the to-do list in less than an hour! No one had to beg us. We are men of honor, and we loved the opportunity to show it to the one God has placed in authority in our lives.

Tragically, often many believers won't even show that type of honor to God.

He is the eternal Creator and we are His creation, and yet He has to beg or command some Christians to do something—and, at that, it needs to be something extremely convenient and beneficial for them to get their "yes." That's because they've forgotten who He is and what He's done.

There is no reason that God should have given His Son as an atoning sacrifice for our sins to restore us to relationship in Him. It was not because He needs us or because we have something that can benefit Him in some way. He is complete in who He is.

He is simply perfect in all His ways—and that is worthy of our respect. There is nothing about any of us that merits Jesus' sacrifice. Christ went to Calvary because He is good and because He is merciful and because He is compassionate, because He had pity on us in our rebellion and brokenness and selfishness. And that is worthy of our respect.

We'll only really appreciate this, however, when we comprehend the full measure of what Yahweh has done for us in saving us. And we can only do that when we get a glimpse of the fearsome holiness that we've been invited to experience by faith in the atoning sacrifice of Christ—where the loving fierceness of God meets the fearsome love of God.

GOD CALLS US FRIENDS, NOT BUDDIES

Another way respect has been devalued is that it has frequently been reduced to meaning just being nice to people: treat everyone like they're your pal, whether it's your boss or the girl at the grocery store checkout.

Not surprisingly, this eroding of a real sense of what honor is has been accompanied by an increasing overfamiliarity inside our churches. I've been shocked at the way I hear some people refer to God, as though He is their homeroom study partner or a teammate on their church league softball team.

We have been called into an intimate, loving relationship with the eternal, infinite Creator of the universe. He not only calls us His children, but we also get to speak to Him familiarly, calling Him *Father*. "For you did not receive the spirit of bondage again to fear, but you received the Spirit of adoption by whom we cry out, 'Abba, Father'" (Rom. 8:15).

That is the same way Jesus addressed the Father when He wrestled over His forthcoming arrest and crucifixion in the Garden of Gethsemane: "Abba, Father, all things are possible for You. Take this cup away from Me; nevertheless, not what I will, but what You will" (Mark 14:36).

And yet, that doesn't mean we should treat God as though He's our college roommate. I've actually heard people pray like, "God, hey, what's up, dude? Love You." I don't think they are going to get struck down by lightning because of it. Surely there is mercy for us all, but the places of greater intimacy require greater maturity. And maturity in God's eyes begins with acknowledgment of God's deity. I fear that without appropriate honor that is born out of healthy, holy fear, people who may use familiar language with God won't ever actually experience the intimacy with Him their words and manner may suggest.

Buddies are a blessing, but they are not usually the highest priority in our lives; we get to them when it's most convenient for us. They exist as an accessory to an otherwise full life. That's not a way to approach our relationship with God if we really want to know Him. He will not share our affections or settle for sitting idly by in the corner of our crowded lives. We must honor Him as Lord.

Important as it is, however, honor in its own strength is only window dressing. Righteous respect is the result of encounter, not the requisite for it. As I have said, you can't respect your way into a fear of the Lord—though, as I'll get into later, it's possible to help create an environment in which we are better able to experience Him in greater depth.

If we show respect only out of a sense of duty, rather than devotion, we are in danger of ending up like the Pharisees. Jesus spoke of them, quoting Isaiah: "These people draw near to Me with their mouth, and honor Me with their lips, but their heart is far from Me. And in vain they worship Me, teaching as doctrines the commandments of men" (Matt. 15:8–9). True respect will naturally flow from people who know the fear of the Lord.

FEAR CAN BE OUR BEST FRIEND

When I speak about how fear can be our best friend, someone will usually quote 1 John 4:18: "There is no fear in love; but perfect love casts out fear, because fear involves torment. But he who fears has not been made perfect in love." How can I square that verse with the claim that fear is a good thing, they want to know.

IF WE SHOW RESPECT ONLY OUT OF A SENSE OF DUTY, RATHER THAN DEVOTION, WE ARE IN DANGER OF ENDING UP LIKE THE PHARISEES.

It's all about being afraid of the right thing, I tell them. God knows that we should have every reason to be afraid of Him. His infinite presence and His total purity inevitably assault every ungenuine thing we may seek to cover or control in our lives. When people in the Bible encountered an angelic being who had been in God's presence, their usual reaction compelled the angel to start the conversation by saying, "Do not be afraid." Think of Gideon, Mary, the shepherds (Judg. 6:23; Luke 1:30; 2:10).

If created beings who have been in God's presence cause that kind of reaction, how much more should God Himself? When we realize how much we have to fear, then we really have reason to be grateful that because of Jesus we no longer need to be fearful!

That sounds like a bit of a paradox, but writing at the Hebrew4Christians website, author John J. Parsons put it like this:

It is the combination of fear and love that leads us to the place of genuine awe. At the Cross, we see God's passionate hatred for sin as well as God's awesome love for sinners. The resurrection of Yeshua represents God's vindicating love. We stand in awe of God because of His love and His righteousness. He is both "just" and the "justifier" of those who are trusting in His salvation.[3]

Some people also point out that 2 Timothy 1:7 says, "For God has not given us a spirit of fear, but of power and of love and of a sound mind." This is another of those times when the translation is inadequate. The Greek word used for fear in this verse is not *phobos*, which we discussed earlier, but *deilia*, which means "cowardice, timidity."

Cowardice is certainly not something God wants for us. And when we appropriately fear Him for who He is—our heavenly Father—we have no reason to ever shrink back from whatever may come, because we know who fights for us. We can face down our fears and laugh in the face of our Brocks.

Fear can be our best friend, if we allow it, drawing us closer to God, or it can be our worst enemy, driving us away. Moses told the Israelites, "Do not fear; for God has come to test you, and that His fear may be before you, so that you may not sin" (Ex. 20:20).

He was saying that right, godly fear would cause them to do the right thing.

I'm struck by the way the same idea is presented in the parable of the talents, told by Jesus (Matthew 25). The master had entrusted his money to three servants when he went away, leaving one with five talents, another with two, and the last with one—each "according to his own ability" (v. 15). When the master came back, the first two reported well on their efforts, each doubling what he had been left with. The master was very pleased with both of them.

Then the third servant came, probably brushing the dirt off the talent he had buried in the ground to keep it safe. The master was not impressed, calling the servant "wicked and lazy" (v. 26). He took the one talent away from that servant and gave it to one of the others, and then "cast the unprofitable servant into . . . outer darkness" (v. 30).

This seems pretty tough, at first sight. But there is a lesson here for us all. The third servant excused his actions by saying that he knew his master to be "a hard man . . . I was afraid," he said (vv. 24–25).

Yet the other two servants must have known the same thing about the master. They were surely also aware of how exacting his standards were. He was not unreasonable, though—he didn't expect more of his servants than he knew each was capable of. Even so, the ones who had been given more talents might have been forgiven for being more nervous about their situation. After all, they knew they'd be called to account for the "more" they'd been given.

The difference between the faithful servants and the "unprofitable" one was that the faithful servants allowed their fear to drive them forward, to be fuel to their fire, causing them to rightly steward what they had been entrusted with. They multiplied what they had been given, earning this awesome commendation: "Well done, good and faithful servant; you have been faithful over a few things, I will make you ruler over many things. Enter into the joy of your lord" (vv. 21, 23).

That is the moment I am living for, when God commends me for my work on earth, and if I can let fear drive me deeper into my devotion to God and His dream, I will find myself positioned and prepared for that glorious moment!

Let's Pray

Yahweh,

Teach me to fear You above all else. There is no one like You!

Deliver me from the common deception of carelessness in Your presence.

I see that fear is fear, and I know that You are a fearsome, wild God!

Teach me to love You even though I can't control You, amen.

CHAPTER 5

MOSES: A MAN WHO FEARED GOD

Now this is the commandment, and these are the
statutes and judgments which the LORD your God
has commanded to teach you . . . that you may fear
the LORD your God, to keep all His statutes and His
commandments . . . that your days may be prolonged.
—DEUTERONOMY 6:1–2

If anyone from the Bible could tell us about the fear of the Lord, it's surely Moses. From his encounter with a strange burning bush, through the destruction of the pursuing Egyptians when the parted Red Sea rushed back in on them, to his weeks up on a mountain wrapped in thick clouds and rocked by lightning and thunder, Moses experienced the wildness and fierceness of a life lived in pursuit of Yahweh Elohim.

Yes, you may be thinking, *but Moses was a mighty man of faith. After all, God spoke to him "face to face, as a man speaks to his friend"* (Ex. 33:11). You're not in the same league, you say.

But remember this: God did not choose Moses because he was a great leader. He chose him because he had a good heart, and then He shaped him into a great leader.

Interestingly, Moses wasn't just born to experience and model the fear of the Lord; he was actually born as a *result* of the fear of the Lord, as if it were part of his very DNA.

In Exodus 1, we read how, after many years of the good life in Egypt, the Israelites were enslaved by a Pharaoh who did not know the story of how they had found shelter and favor there through Joseph. Seeing how numerous they were, Pharaoh feared they might join with Egypt's enemies one day. So he "set taskmasters over them to afflict them with their burdens" (v. 11).

That didn't seem to work, however, and the Israelites continued to multiply. So then Pharaoh ordered the Hebrew midwives to kill any male babies they might help to deliver. But "the midwives *feared* God, and did not do as the king of Egypt commanded them, but saved the male children alive" (v. 17, emphasis added).

Not only do we see in this account how the fear of God can inspire people to do the right thing even in the face of grave danger, but we also discover the rewards that can follow.

When Pharaoh asked the midwives why they weren't dealing with the male babies as he had ordered, they spun a story about how "lively" the Israelite women were (v. 19), claiming they delivered before the midwives could reach them.

"Therefore God dealt well with the midwives, and the people multiplied and grew very mighty. And so it was, *because the midwives feared God,* that He provided households for them" (vv. 20–21, emphasis added).

It was through the fear of the Lord that the man who would deliver God's people from oppression was born. But it wouldn't be until he experienced that fear for himself that he would be able to step into that role.

When we meet Moses in Exodus 3, he is a forgotten, frightened runaway. Raised in Pharaoh's house, he had tried to intervene when he saw an Israelite slave being mistreated, killing the Egyptian overseer. While his concern may have been admirable, the way he went about things was a mess. Not only did he alienate the Israelites he'd intended to help (Ex. 2:13–14), but he also ended up with a bounty on his head.

The onetime prince of Egypt fled to Midian and spent the next forty years hiding out in the desert as a lowly shepherd. And so we come to the first of seven episodes in Moses' life that reveal something about the fear of the Lord to us.

THE FUTURE: FINDING DIRECTION
THROUGH THE FEAR OF THE LORD

Did Moses ever wonder how things were going for his people back in Egypt? Did he want to know whether his "wanted" poster was still hanging in all the post offices back there? Or had he forgotten his people's pitiful state and his desire to do something about it?

That's not clear from Scripture, but what we do know is that God had not forgotten. He heard the Israelites' groaning "and God remembered His covenant with Abraham, with Isaac, and with Jacob. And God looked upon the children of Israel, and God acknowledged them" (Ex. 2:24–25).

And then He caused a bush in the desert to burst into flames.

A burning bush that didn't get consumed must have been an

intriguing, even scary sight. We're not given any dimensions in Exodus 3, but I am guessing it must have been fairly sizable, certainly large enough to attract Moses' attention. Not just a nice, cozy hearth-size fire.

And the whole encounter must have been pretty incredible when you consider that at the end, God sent Moses back to Egypt—to the source of his fear and his failure and his shame—and he went. Moses would repeatedly confront Pharaoh, despite the warrant out for his arrest and his reputation as a murderer.

Only something greater than the shame he had experienced in Egypt could have compelled Moses and given him the confidence to return. Indeed, the fear of God gave Moses the strength to face his own fears.

There's a lesson in Moses' back-of-the-desert encounter for anyone wanting to pursue God more closely: you may not get to hear God speak to you where you are right now. Moses said to himself, "I must *turn aside* now and see this marvelous sight, why the bush is not burned up" (Ex. 3:3 NASB, emphasis added). Only after that did God speak to him from the burning bush.

Moses left where he was and went to where God was moving. Perhaps you need to do the same.

I was talking with a young woman one time who was caught up in drugs, living with her dealer in a cheap hotel. "I know that I want to get right with God," she told me, "I just don't know where He wants me."

"Of course you don't," I told her. "You don't even know how to hear God's voice. If you want to hear God speaking, you can start by going to where you can see God moving."

For her, that meant leaving her living situation and going to Bible college in Dallas. I was able to find a place for her at a school where, soon enough, God began to speak to her regarding her identity and His purpose for her life. Now she hears His voice clearly, is walking in His ways, and is telling others about Him. She actually lives now in Mobile, Alabama, near me and my family, and is an awesome part of our community and a blessing to everyone she meets.

Too many Christians who quietly yearn for more of God think they can just keep doing what they've been doing and God will demand their attention if He really needs it. But if you're looking for identity and for purpose, for an assignment and a calling, you may need to "turn aside" and go find some "holy ground" on which to listen to God's voice (Ex. 3:3–5).

How might you do that? Find people who are on fire! Maybe there's a church, a conference, or a Bible study you know of where a fire is burning. Check it out, even if the adjustment is inconvenient, and you may find God speaking to you there.

Be prepared to take off your shoes, as Moses did. After he responded to the fire and God's voice, he was told, "Take your sandals off your feet, for the place where you stand is holy ground" (v. 5).

This order wasn't just about a dress code. This was God telling Moses that he was coming to a different place, and that he was going to have to walk differently. No doubt, when Moses slipped off his sandals, he watched where he put his feet on the rough desert ground.

In the same way, the fear of God will cause us to walk differently, gingerly, thoughtfully. When we encounter God in the fire, we find ourselves on holy ground. In Hebrew the word for holy is *kadesh*, which means "set apart." If we really want to know God's holy place, we will set ourselves to walk in a holy way—set apart from the way things used to be.

That means all that we are and everything we have. We'll be careful not only where we place our feet, but also where we position our ears and eyes as we consume media, and where we put our time and money.

FREEDOM: DELIVERANCE THROUGH
THE FEAR OF THE LORD

Sometimes Bible stories are so familiar to us that we can almost end up treating them like fairy tales if we are not careful. Cute, but not to be taken too seriously. But when we allow ourselves to consider the reality of what happened in those stories, we get a clearer picture of God, His nature, and His ways.

THE FEAR OF GOD WILL CAUSE US TO WALK DIFFERENTLY, GINGERLY, THOUGHTFULLY.

That's certainly true of Moses' encounters with Pharaoh and the Passover story.

Reading between the lines, the series of escalating clashes between Moses and Pharaoh's magicians was pretty scary. There was clearly something otherworldly going on: staffs turning into snakes, the water of the Nile turning into blood. Just imagine the stench.

And then, finally, the brutal climax at Passover. In our jubilation at the Israelites' freedom, we tend to overlook how it came about. Remember that as the Israelites sheltered under their blood-marked doorposts, the angel of death came and took the life of every single Egyptian firstborn, humans and animals alike (Ex. 11:4–6).

Think about it: thousands of Egyptian parents woke in the morning to find still, lifeless children. Why? Because they were enemies of God.

But it didn't end there. In addition to nationwide grief, there was likely great hardship too. The crops had already been devastated by the plagues; now the livestock was decimated. And on top of that, a frightened Pharaoh ordered the Israelites out of his country. The Egyptians' long-time source of free labor went with them.

As grateful as the Israelites were for God's goodness to them in freeing them from slavery, they were well aware that His love for them was invariably connected to anger toward their captors. God Himself even reminded them of that later. When Moses went up on Mount Sinai to meet with God, he was instructed to "tell the children of Israel: 'You have seen what I did to the Egyptians'" (Ex. 19:3–4).

Through godly fear, Moses became the deliverer of his people. But have you ever wondered why God chose him for the task? He was a runaway murderer, after all. Not much of a candidate, it would seem. Part of the reason, I believe, was that he was the only one who knew the way out. After all, in recorded history to that point, he was the only Israelite to ever get up and walk out of Egypt!

Think about that in relation to people you may know—family, friends, coworkers, loved ones, neighbors. As someone who has experienced deliverance through Christ, you have the opportunity to go back to those who are still enslaved in sin and shame and tell them, "Hey, guess what! I know the way out of captivity, and His name is Jesus!"

FORCE: MOVED TO RIGHT LIVING BY THE FEAR OF THE LORD

With the ten plagues and the Passover fresh in their minds, and the terrifying ways God had dealt with His enemies, it's perhaps not surprising that the Israelites told Moses, "All that the LORD has spoken we will do" (Ex. 19:8). They wanted to be on the right side. Fear and gratitude spurred them to obedience.

God's motive is relationship, not just rules. He didn't give the Israelites the Ten Commandments and then scare them into trying to keep them. He showed them His awesomeness and fearfulness first, a glimpse of His amazing might and magnitude, and then He told them how they should live as a result.

It is so important that we get this in the right order. Otherwise a relationship with God becomes something we try to live up to, to earn, rather than something we strive to live out, to experience.

By the time they got to Sinai, the Israelites had already seen God's awesome power, of course, but it had been directed at others. When Moses went up the mountain to meet with God, they got a glimpse of it for themselves, and it was frightening: "Then it came to pass on the third day, in the morning, that there were thunderings and lightnings, and a thick cloud on the mountain; and the sound of the trumpet was very loud, so that all the people who were in the camp *trembled*" (Ex. 19:16).

In the following verses, we read that the mountain was covered in smoke because the Lord had descended upon it in fire, with the heat of a furnace. The whole mountain quaked. Remarkably, God told Moses to go down the mountain and warn the people not to come closer, lest they die. For me, I think sheer terror would have overcome any curiosity, and I would have been running in the opposite direction!

In the next chapter, we discover God's reason for giving the Israelites this glimpse of His glory. Moses gave them the Ten Commandments that Yahweh had spoken up on the mountain. But they were scared.

> Now all the people witnessed the thunderings, the lightning flashes, the sound of the trumpet, and the mountain smoking; and when the people saw it, they trembled and stood afar off. Then they said to Moses, "You speak with us, and we will hear; but let not God speak with us, lest we die." (Ex. 20:18–19)

In his answer to them, Moses got to the heart of it all: "Do not fear; for God has come to test you, and that His fear may be *before* you, so that you may not sin" (v. 20).

This is one of the times the Hebrew word used for fear is *yare'*, meaning "scared" or "frightened," not "awe." In other words, "Don't be scared away. Be scared near." This is God's strategy for dealing with sin. If you have the fear of the Lord before you, in front of you, it's like a protective barrier between you and sin. Knowing how all-consuming God is, we will think twice about lightly disobeying what He says. When we are so fixed on Him, sin can come calling and we won't even hear the doorbell ring.

That almost sounds like an oversimplification, but it's not. It is that simple—though simple doesn't necessarily mean easy. Training for a marathon involves running a bit farther each time. Simple, but definitely not easy. You have to be dedicated, determined, and disciplined.

When it's boiled down to its most fundamental form, sin means that for a moment I took my eyes off God. It's like Peter, when he was walking on water. He was fine until he looked away from Jesus and focused on the waves.

But if we are truly walking in the fear of the Lord, we will be moved to *right living*, not to sin.

FURY: CONFRONTING COMPROMISE WITH THE FEAR OF THE LORD

Maybe you have heard the story about the church that regularly held old-time revival services. Each time one guy in the congregation would run down to the altar at some stage, shouting, "Fill me, Jesus! Fill me, Jesus!"

Finally, after he had done the same thing over and over again, an old lady at the back of the church shouted out, "Don't do it, Lord! He leaks!"

Isn't that the truth? We can have a powerful encounter with God but then find ourselves soon drifting back into our old ways. That was never more true than of the Israelites. If anyone had experienced God in dramatic fashion, they had. They had survived the plagues He brought on Egypt, seen His deliverance in the Passover, and watched as He swept the Egyptian army away in the Red Sea. Then they'd trembled as Mount Sinai quaked at God's presence, and they promised to do all that He said.

How long did it take for that sense of God's awesome might to fade, for them to lose that zeal? Just a few weeks. Moses went up on the mountain with God for six weeks, and in that short a time, the Israelites got restless:

> Now when the people saw that Moses delayed coming down from the mountain, the people gathered together to Aaron, and said to him, "Come, make us gods that shall go before us; for as for this Moses, the man who brought us up out of the land of Egypt, we do not know what has become of him." (Ex. 32:1)

How did they handle the waiting, the uncertainty? They went back to what was familiar. The idea of a golden calf wasn't something they just pulled out of the air. It was a reminder of their life in Egypt, where there were several bull cults.[1] Having seen God in so many unfamiliar ways, the Israelites wanted something known, something predictable, something they considered safe. They tried to make God manageable, turn Him into something that looked like all the other gods, so they could deal with Him the way other people did with their gods.

They didn't pack up and go all the way back to Egypt. That would have been too obvious. They just tried to make where they were a bit more like the land they had just come out of.

I believe we are prone to doing the same thing in the church. Rather than wait on God for what He has, we revert to what we know, to what we are comfortable with. We may not walk into flagrant rebellion, but we tend to choose quiet compromise.

It's also why you can go into many churches and they seem more like places of entertainment than houses of worship, because we're trying to make them look like Egypt rather than the holy mountain. We choose the carnal over the presence of God in an effort to make the church look more like the world to attract worldly minded people. We should be making the church look more like heaven to attract heaven-hungry people.

The Israelites should not have been surprised at how God reacted to their idolatry. He had already told them through Moses, "I, the LORD your God, am a jealous God" (Ex. 20:5). Yet they had intentionally sinned.

Note that the people had not "strayed" or "stumbled," as we like to put it sometimes. To God, they had "corrupted themselves" (Ex. 32:7). How? The next verse tells us: "They have turned aside quickly out of the way which I commanded them" (v. 8).

God was so angry that had Moses not interceded, He would have consumed them. Had He done so, He would have been perfectly just in His actions, as extreme as it might sound to us. God relented, but there were still severe consequences. The sons of Levi killed three thousand of the people who were worshiping the golden calf, and God sent a plague on the rest (vv. 28, 35).

This is how seriously He views idolatry. We may not bow down to statues these days, but we do give other things the place in our life that God demands, from material comfort to mass entertainment.

God has no time or room for compromise. You can't hold on to sin with one hand and the Savior with the other. The two are going in different directions, and you will be torn apart.

FIRE: KNOWING GOD THROUGH THE FEAR OF THE LORD

One of the biggest mistakes we can make as Christians is to put more emphasis on serving God than on knowing Him. If we are not careful, we can spend more time praying and studying to increase our productivity rather than deepening our intimacy.

The truth is, though, the world will be more impacted by how we are changed in our time with God than by what we learn in it. There's that old saying that real, living faith is caught, not taught.

Moses seemed to know this. Since being called to lead the Israelites to freedom, he had confronted Pharaoh, organized the exodus, delivered the Ten Commandments, and rebuked the people for worshiping the golden calf.

But he knew that God's directions were not enough. He told God, "If Your Presence does not go with us, do not bring us up from here. For how then will it be known that Your people and I have found grace in Your sight, except You go with us? So we shall be separate, Your people and I, from all the people who are upon the face of the earth" (Ex. 33:15–16).

Moses was aware it was not just what he and the people did that would set them apart from the nations around them. He wanted more: "Please, show me Your glory" (v. 18). Even when God warned that no one could see His face and live, Moses was not deterred.

God answered his cry. He told Moses, "Here is a place by Me, and you shall stand on the rock. So it shall be, while My glory passes by, that I will put you in the cleft of the rock, and will cover you with My hand while I pass by. Then I will take away My hand, and you shall see My back; but My face shall not be seen" (vv. 21–23).

God had already revealed Himself to Moses through the burning bush, which was amazing enough. Then He visited with Moses on the mountain and spoke with him "face to face, as a man speaks to his friend" in the tent of meeting (v. 11). But this encounter was even closer.

What must that experience have been like? Much like the action movie scene I mentioned earlier, I imagine, in which the hero just escapes as an inferno rushes past and over him. Wonderful and fearful.

It was so impactful that Moses didn't need to tell anyone about it. They just knew something had happened. When he came down the mountain, Moses "did not know that the skin of his face shone while he talked with Him" (Ex. 34:29). In fact, people were so freaked out that they were afraid to get too close to him, and he had to wear a veil over his face.

I'm reminded of the story I heard about the famous evangelist Charles Finney. He prayed for several weeks to be saved, not wanting to treat such a moment lightly. He would go out into the woods to be alone with God, crying out to know Him.

In due time he had a profound encounter with God, which he would later describe as like having liquid love wash over him. As he walked back into the city, people could tell just by looking at Finney that something had happened to him—and they were so intrigued that some of them ran into the woods to try to find out what had happened there.

Like Moses and Finney, I want my relationship with God to be grounded in experience, in encounter. I don't want to just know about God; I want to know Him. I want my theology to be the explanation of my faith, not the reason for it.

I want to see the people of God have a heart of desperate pursuit, as Moses did, even though the closer you get, the more you can feel the heat, and the brighter the light is, the more violently the earth shakes—still saying yes to all that even in spite of the risk. If we would do that, we would finally come to a place where God's Word is not only our worldview, but our defining characteristic. And we would not simply give a testimony to the world around us; we would become a testimony to the world around us.

FORGETTING: LOOKING AHEAD IN
THE FEAR OF THE LORD

When the fear of the Lord is before us, in front of us, as God wants it to be, it lights the way for us. The psalmist wrote, "Your word is a lamp to my feet and a light to my path" (Ps. 119:105).

However, when we let the fear of the Lord fall behind us—that is, we forget to fear Him—we block out part of its light. If it has to shine over our shoulder, as it were, it can cast a shadow. And the wrong kind of fears lurk in the shadows.

The story of the twelve spies is an important reminder of what happens when we forget the fear of the Lord. We give in to the giants ahead of us.

When the Israelites reached the Wilderness of Paran, God told Moses to send out a representative from each of the twelve tribes to spy out the promised land ahead of them. God knew what was there, because through Moses He warned the spies to "be of good courage" (Num. 13:20). Unfortunately, they seemed to ignore this advice.

Returning from their exploratory trip, they showed some of the juicy grapes they had gathered and reported that the land did flow with milk and honey, just as God had promised. Nevertheless, they went on: "The people who dwell in the land are strong; the cities are fortified and very large; moreover we saw the descendants of Anak there. The Amalekites dwell in the land of the South; the Hittites, the Jebusites, and the Amorites dwell in the mountains; and the Canaanites dwell by the sea and along the banks of the Jordan" (vv. 28–29).

When Caleb tried to encourage the people that they were capable of overcoming any adversary, the ten spies who brought back the discouraging report insisted, "We are not able to go up against the people, for they are stronger than we" (v. 31).

The consequences were massive. The Israelites put the plagues of judgment against the Egyptians, the punishment of the Passover, and the parting of the Red Sea—evidence of a fearful God—behind them. As a result, the giants in front of them seemed to tower.

The Israelites' failure to go into the promised land wasn't just a lack of faith. It was rebellion. Moses told them:

> Nevertheless you would not go up, but rebelled against the command of the LORD your God; and you complained in your tents, and said, "Because the LORD hates us, He has brought us out of the land of Egypt to deliver us into the hand of the Amorites, to destroy us. Where can we go up? Our brethren have discouraged our hearts, saying, 'The people are greater and taller than we; the cities are great and fortified up to heaven; moreover we have seen the sons of the Anakim there.'"
>
> Then I said to you, "Do not be terrified, or afraid of them. The LORD your God, who goes before you, He will fight for you, according to all He did for you in Egypt before your eyes, and in the wilderness where you saw how the LORD your God carried you, as a man carries his son, in all the way that you went until you came to this place." Yet, for all that, you did not believe the LORD your God. (Deut. 1:26–32)

The result? An entire generation—except for Caleb and Joshua, the two spies who came back confident that God could do what He had promised—failed to enter into all that God had for them.

Have you known God's mighty power in the past, but right now you're facing giants that seem too much, too big? Marriage problems? Addiction? Keep the fear of the Lord in front of you. After all, He will fight for you—and He never loses.

FAITHFULNESS: ACKNOWLEDGING
AUTHORITY IN THE FEAR OF THE LORD

You may not always be able to tell if someone is living in the fear of the Lord because his or her face shines, as Moses' did, but you can get a good idea from the way that person talks about the church.

As I've mentioned, I believe that in many cases and places, we have made the church into a golden calf. We have tried to "Egyptify" our faith. We run churches the way we run businesses, with boards and branding and focus groups, because we're more comfortable with the culture of captivity than we are with the culture of heaven.

I don't see God building a franchise in the Bible, however. I see Him building a kingdom; I see Him establishing a family. Kingdoms have authority, and families have love that doesn't quit. They both require loyalty, and God doesn't take it lightly when His ways are ignored, even for apparently spiritual reasons. Maybe especially so.

Look at what happened when Korah led a rebellion against Moses and Aaron. He gathered a group to complain, alleging that the brothers were setting themselves up above everyone else: "You take too much upon yourselves, for all the congregation is holy, every one of them, and the LORD is among them. Why then do you exalt yourselves above the assembly of the LORD?" (Num. 16:3).

Korah and his followers thought they were being godly. They didn't have anything against God, or so they believed; they just felt that Moses and Aaron were getting a bit too big for their britches. But they failed to realize that in rejecting those God had placed in leadership over them, they were, in fact, rejecting Him.

Moses was well aware of this, that it wasn't about his position but about God. When he warned the people to step away from the tents of Korah and his group, because he knew the ground was going to open up to swallow them, he told them, "Then you will understand that these men have rejected the LORD" (v. 30). Notice that he did not say they had rejected him as leader, but that they had rejected the God who had set him in leadership.

Not only did Korah and those close to him perish, so did 250 other men who had sided with him and who had offered incense. They were consumed by a fire that "came out from the LORD" (v. 35). Amazingly, the people still didn't get it. The next day they rose up against Moses and Aaron, claiming that the men had "killed the people of the LORD" (Num. 16:41). In response, God sent a plague that killed almost fifteen thousand people.

Let's not gloss over this. They died because they resisted God's authority. He does not take the rejection of His declared order lightly by any means. When Samuel confronted King Saul for failing to destroy all the Amalekites, as he had been instructed, the prophet told him, "Rebellion is as the sin of witchcraft, and stubbornness is as iniquity and idolatry" (1 Sam. 15:23).

FAMILIARITY: FINISHING WELL IN THE FEAR OF THE LORD

How is it that we seem to read so often about people who have served God faithfully and well for years, but who end up falling away somehow later on? What's going on here?

I suspect they may have become guilty of coasting. They began to think that because they have "done well" for so long, they could afford to ease off the gas a little, not press into God so hard. Take things a bit easy. But God doesn't give us a pass because of past performance. That lesson can clearly be seen in Moses' life. When the Israelites got to the Wilderness of Zin, they found there was no water. Once again they began grumbling.

After seeking God's direction, Moses was given specific instructions: "Take the rod; you and your brother Aaron gather the congregation together. Speak to the rock before their eyes, and it will yield its water; thus you shall bring water for them out of the rock, and give drink to the congregation and their animals" (Num. 20:8).

Then Moses gathered the people, lifted his rod—and made a terrible mistake. Rather than do what God had said this time, speak to the rock, he did what God had said previously. Three chapters earlier, the Israelites had also been complaining that there was no water. When Moses cried out to God then, he was instructed to take the staff he had held up to part the Nile when they fled the Egyptians and strike the rock at Horeb (Ex. 17:6). He did so, and life-giving water flowed for all the people.

Fast-forward to the same situation a while later, and Moses half-way obeyed. Some say he struck the rock with his staff because he was angry at the people's complaining. Personally, I think it was because he was only half listening. He remembered what had worked the last time; it was familiar to him. He figured that the same approach would work this time. He had also become familiar with God, so he didn't really tune in to the specifics of what God had said.

Isn't that so true of the church today? We find something that works, and we keep doing it. Someone strikes the rock, you might say, and then writes a book explaining how others can do the same thing or holds seminars about how to do it. There are whole denominations that are still doing things the way they did back in 1967, or whenever, because it worked that way then. Hitting the rock as if it's ten, fifty, or a hundred years ago.

Though Moses didn't do things the way he had been directed, God still let the life-giving water come. That was a sign of His mercy and kindness, and He still does the same today. People are saved and touched and healed even where the church is stuck in the past, not because we are doing what He's commanded, but because He is good.

There were serious consequences for Moses' disobedience, however. God told him, "Because you did not believe Me, to hallow Me in the eyes of the children of Israel, therefore you shall not bring this assembly into the land which I have given them" (Num. 20:12).

This was not God being petty. Moses had failed to "hallow" God, honoring Him as holy in front of the people. Fear had been replaced by familiarity. This should be a sobering reminder for anyone at any level of leadership. Don't presume that just because something worked last week, last month, or last year, it's what God has in mind for today.

When I speak on leadership, I always warn, "Don't marry the method." We have to be totally committed to doing what God says to do *today*, even if it seems unorthodox or unfamiliar. Joy Dawson has a sobering view of what that really means:

> The fear of God is evidenced in our lives by instant, joyful and whole obedience to God. That is biblical obedience. Anything else is disobedience. Delayed obedience is disobedience. Partial obedience is disobedience. Doing what God has asked with murmuring is disobedience.[2]

We all want to finish well, don't we? Then let's not become so familiar with God that we fail to listen to even His still, small voice.

Let's Pray

Father,

I long to encounter You like Your friend Moses did.

Mark me for Your glory, and use me to do Your purposes in the earth.

I pray for a greater measure of encounter that would lead me, like Moses, into a greater measure of strength, amen.

CHAPTER 6

PENTECOST: THE CHURCH BIRTHED IN FIRE, FEAR, FELLOWSHIP

My name is to be feared among the nations.

—MALACHI 1:14

Many Christians believe in God 2.0. They seem to think that He has been revised and updated, like a software program, and they quite like the new version. The earlier one, not so much. They may not actually put it quite like this, perhaps, but in effect they view Jesus as sort of a patch, having fixed the bugs in the launch edition. They divide the Bible into two halves—the Old Testament "angry God," and the New Testament "loving God."

This old-God, new-God thinking isn't a recent development, but it's gotten more widespread lately, especially as people increasingly reject the idea of absolutes and declare that truth is subjective. You need an easygoing God with that kind of worldview.

But it couldn't be more wrong. God did not change His mind along the way. He did not come to the conclusion that He needed a softer image, that maybe He should lighten up a little on some stuff. He didn't decide to turn a blind eye to a few things so people would be more likely to accept Him.

The fear of the Lord that we've traced through the pages of the Old Testament, as seen in the life of Moses, is woven just as strongly through the life of the early church as recorded in the pages of the New Testament, if we have eyes to see. In fact, *phobos*, the Greek word used for fear in the New Testament, occurs there forty-seven times—that's six times more than the word for fear, *yare'*, that is in the Old Testament.

The fear of the Lord is actually one of the defining characteristics of the early church. It's as much a part of Pentecost as signs and wonders. It's one vital thread in the three-strand cord that God wove into the newborn church: fire, fear, fellowship.

Think about how it began. Jesus had ascended into heaven, telling His disciples not to depart from Jerusalem, but to "wait for the Promise of the Father, 'which,' He said, 'you have heard from Me; for John truly baptized with water, but you shall be baptized with the Holy Spirit not many days from now'" (Acts 1:4–5).

> THE FEAR OF THE LORD IS ACTUALLY ONE OF THE DEFINING CHARACTERISTICS OF THE EARLY CHURCH.

This shouldn't have been a complete surprise to the disciples. Back before His arrest and execution, Jesus had told them, "Nevertheless I tell you the truth. It is to your advantage that I go away; for if I do not go away, the Helper will not come to you; but if I depart, I will send Him to you" (John 16:7).

This Holy Spirit encounter wasn't going to be just some kind of symbolic thing either. Jesus told His followers that they would "receive power when the Holy Spirit has come upon you" (Acts 1:8). The Greek word used for power here is *dunamis*, from which we get the word *dynamite*. In other words, something explosive and unmistakable was going to happen to them.

Still, it may have been hard for the disciples to believe that Jesus' going away was a good thing. Surely at least some of them must have been thinking, *We could do anything if we only had You standing next to us, Jesus.* I have to admit, I sometimes feel the same way. If I had a flesh-and-blood Jesus standing next to me, I don't think there's anything I wouldn't do.

I'd go down to the children's hospital and clear that out, for starters. Heal them up and send them home. Then I'd go to every jail and every crack house and proclaim true, total freedom to the captives. Next, I'd visit every mental hospital and speak peace and a sound mind to the afflicted. With Jesus by my side, I'd be unstoppable, I think. And yet He said that, no, it was *better* that He left His disciples because then the Holy Spirit could come. And how true His words became:

> When the Day of Pentecost had fully come, they were all with one accord in one place. And suddenly there came a sound from heaven, as of a rushing mighty wind, and it filled the whole house where they were sitting. Then there appeared to them divided tongues, as of fire, and one sat upon each of them. And they were all filled with the Holy Spirit and began to speak with other tongues, as the Spirit gave them utterance. (Acts 2:1–4)

This was a scary moment! Glowing tongues of fires came to rest on their heads—the same fire that burned in the bush in front of Moses, the same fire that consumed the altar on the top of Mount Carmel when Elijah called out to God (1 Kings 18).

This was the same fire John the Baptist had spoken of: "I indeed baptize you with water unto repentance, but He who is coming after me is mightier than I, whose sandals I am not worthy to carry. He will baptize you with the Holy Spirit and fire" (Matt. 3:11).

The results were amazing. The disciples, who had been meeting behind closed doors because they were scared of what might happen to them, spilled out into the streets. Some of those who had crowded into Jerusalem began to make fun of the disciples, saying they were drunk. But the disciples were not intimidated. Peter not only stood up and denied that he and the others were drunk, but he also preached a fiery sermon. This was the same disciple who only a short time before had denied he even knew Jesus the night He was arrested and taken before Caiaphas the high priest.

Surely his fear of man had been burned away, replaced with a confident fear of the living God. Peter declared boldly, "This Jesus God has raised up, of which we are all witnesses. Therefore being exalted to the right hand of God, and having received from the Father the promise of the Holy Spirit, He poured out this which you now see and hear . . . Therefore let all the house of Israel know assuredly that God has made this Jesus, whom you crucified, both Lord and Christ" (Acts 2:32–33, 36).

Now consider the result of Peter's unapologetic message. Those listening "were cut to the heart," and said to Peter and the rest of the apostles, "Men and brethren, what shall we do?" (v. 37).

He told them, "Repent, and let every one of you be baptized in the name of Jesus Christ for the remission of sins; and you shall receive the gift of the Holy Spirit. For the promise is to you and to your children, and to all who are afar off, as many as the Lord our God will call" (vv. 38–39).

There is something else for us in the contemporary church to catch in this remarkable event. I believe it shows us that a true, Spirit-filled move of God will inevitably lead to the gospel being preached powerfully and to souls being saved. This is a simple litmus test for an authentic work of God.

A CHURCH BIRTHED IN HOLY FIRE

Far too often in the charismatic movement we say, "Wow! The Holy Spirit is really moving," and we fall on the ground and we cry and we have these wonderful moments; we prophesy back and forth to one another—and then we regain our composure, straighten our clothing, and we walk back out into the world as if nothing ever happened.

At the very best, we may invite some people to come along to this upper room where some wild things are happening. But here, in Jerusalem, as the church was birthed in holy fire, the believers went out to the lost.

And what an impact: three thousand were added to the disciples' numbers in that one day. Incredible. Something had come upon these disciples that was unable to be ignored, explained away, or refuted by those who saw it. It made them relentless, focused, and fearless—and it is just as available to us today as it was to them then.

At Pentecost, there was no question that something supernatural was happening. Acts 2 goes on: "And they continued steadfastly in the apostles' doctrine and fellowship, in the breaking of bread, and in prayers. Then *fear* came upon every soul, and many wonders and signs were done through the apostles" (vv. 42–43).

The Greek word used here is *phobos*. The people weren't wowed or awed or touched by what God was doing in their midst; they were fearful. That, in turn, impacted how they lived:

> Now all who believed were together, and had all things in common,
> and sold their possessions and goods, and divided them among all,
> as anyone had need. So continuing daily with one accord in the

temple, and breaking bread from house to house, they ate their food with gladness and simplicity of heart, praising God and having favor with all the people. And the Lord added to the church daily those who were being saved. (vv. 44–47)

I love to see how this holy fear of God and all that He was doing in their midst shaped the believers' lives. They knew that what was happening was not something caused by their own efforts, but that it was the power from on high that Jesus had promised. They understood what they had been given was not to be taken for granted or taken lightly. They did not consider that they had just become part of a special club; they knew they had been made into an enduring family.

The confidence this fear gave the disciples continued to embolden them, and the church grew by leaps and bounds. Healing a lame man in the temple created a commotion, which Peter used to call people to repentance. Five thousand of them responded, according to Acts 4:4. What amazing church growth. First, three thousand at Pentecost, now five thousand more. These were all men, so with women and children, too, the young church had probably gone from a handful to more than ten thousand in just a matter of days.

After healing the lame man and preaching about the resurrection, Peter and John were arrested and taken before the high priest and the other leaders—the very people in front of whom Peter had denied Jesus on the night He was arrested. But now Peter spoke fearlessly about Jesus. And "when they saw the boldness of Peter and John, and perceived that they were uneducated and untrained men, they marveled. And they realized that they had been with Jesus" (v. 13).

Though they were threatened and told not to keep preaching about Jesus, Peter and John didn't even consider that an option. They didn't go back home to think about it for a while. They prayed that God would "grant to Your servants that with all boldness they may speak Your word, by stretching out Your hand to heal, and that signs and wonders may be done through the name of Your holy Servant Jesus" (vv. 29–30). No more fear of man. Just fire, fellowship, and the fear of God.

STAYING BALANCED AND GIVING UP CONTROL

If the church of Pentecost sat on a three-legged stool formed of fire, fear, and fellowship, many churches today are a bit wobbly because they are missing one of those legs.

There are plenty of churches where there's fellowship and fear, but no fire. People show up regularly, they read their Bibles, and they try to make sure they avoid going to hell by doing the "right" things. But there's no fire compelling them to go and tell others about Jesus—or any real sense of His presence that would touch anyone who did go.

Then there are churches where it's all fire and fellowship, but no fear. Everyone is just kind of floating around, enjoying God's presence, but there's no sense of awe at who He is, no honor of the protocol of His presence, or any desperation to live in a way that pleases Him.

And finally, there are churches where there's plenty of fire and fear but no fellowship. There is passionate pursuit of God, but it's solo and separate. Each person is off by himself or herself, not open to the accountability or vulnerability that only comes in a committed community.

Just as we need a balanced relationship with all three aspects of God's personhood—Father, Son, and Holy Spirit—so we also need to experience the fullness of fear, fire, and fellowship if we are to be more like the New Testament church. As I read Acts, I see a cycle of godly fear and godly power. As God's people walked in the fear of the Lord, God released more power through them, and as God released more power through them, they were all struck again with the fear of the Lord.

This church thing was all new to them, of course, so maybe they were more open to God's moving. We, meanwhile, have years of doing church a certain way, so when God comes wanting to do things differently, it can be a bit threatening. It means letting go of control and being willing to make people uncomfortable.

We were in Oklahoma City for a For Today show when a young woman asked us to pray for her. A special-ed teacher, she'd been head-butted by a student, which had sent splinters of bone into her eyes. As a result, she was blind in one eye and quickly losing her sight in the other.

We'd seen God answer prayers in some remarkable ways before, but I was pretty intimidated. What if we prayed and nothing happened? But as we gathered around the young woman in a preshow group, I reminded myself that this was about her need and God's power and love, not my reputation.

The next few minutes it felt as though we were back in the time of the book of Acts. Candice was the first to pray for the young woman, who reported she could now detect colors and shapes in her blind eye. Encouraged, we huddled around and prayed once more. After her tears subsided, the woman asked a friend to pass her his driver's license. He did, and she burst into tears again as she examined it and announced, "I can see!"

As you might imagine, I felt like I was on cloud nine when I hit the stage that night. During the set I told the crowd some of what had happened and how awesome God was. There were some blank faces—this was a non-Christian venue, after all—but the reaction I got after the show was worse.

A member of one of the other bands on the same tour sought me out backstage. He told me that he was a Christian, too, but you would not have guessed so from the language he used. He told me in no uncertain terms that he thought what I'd said was nonsense, that God didn't do that kind of stuff anymore, and he asked why I was trying to draw attention to myself. He really let me have it.

If I'd been able to get a word in, I'd have invited him to walk over and meet the woman, who was still there at the venue, to hear the story directly from her. But my attacker was having none of it. He just wanted to unload on me and leave.

Sadly, this is not a completely uncommon reaction when God moves in ways beyond our comfort zone. It's not the fear of the Lord; it's more like a fear of the fear of the Lord.

A CAUTIONARY ENCOUNTER

While the accounts of the early days of the church offer an inspiring invitation to walk in the fear of the Lord and the power of the Holy Spirit, they also include a sobering reminder of the seriousness of doing so. The story of Ananias and Sapphira should give us all reason to tread very carefully. This couple sold something to give to the work of the church, but they misrepresented their actions.

Peter called the husband to account: "Ananias, why has Satan filled your heart to lie to the Holy Spirit and keep back part of the price of the land for yourself? While it remained, was it not your own? And after it was sold, was it not in your own control? Why have you conceived this thing in your heart? You have not lied to men but to God" (Acts 5:3–4).

On hearing this, Ananias fell down dead, and "great fear came upon all those who heard these things" (v. 5). When Sapphira came to Peter a little later, she also lied about what she and Ananias had given, with the same fatal result. Perhaps not surprisingly, we read that "great fear came upon all the church and upon all who heard these things" (v. 11).

This, remember, was the loving, merciful New Testament God! But He does not take it lightly when we are dishonest in our dealings with Him and His family. What happened to Ananias and Sapphira causes me to think carefully about all that I do and say. After all, what was their sin? It wasn't so much the money they withheld; it was the impression they were trying to make. They wanted others to think they had given all the proceeds of their sale, when they hadn't. They had held something back.

If I am honest, there are times when I have been just like them. This isn't just about money; it's about wanting to be seen as something more than we really are. Maybe, like me, there have been times when you've slacked off a bit in your devotion to God. You've not studied the Scriptures diligently for a while, you've been a bit half-hearted in your prayer life, but you've pretended that you're still burning strong.

Why is this so important? Because it undermines the purity of the fellowship, the sense of family that God desires for His people, and in so doing it smothers the fire of the Holy Spirit.

I'm just grateful that God has not dealt with me the same way that He did with Ananias and Sapphira in the times I have been half-hearted. That's only His mercy and kindness. Knowing both His great love and His fierceness, I don't want to be like Ananias and Sapphira and one day have to admit, "I held something back."

There is going to be a day, however, when we will all be called to account. The apostle Paul wrote:

> Therefore we make it our aim, whether present or absent, to be well pleasing to Him. For we must all appear before the judgment seat of Christ, that each one may receive the things done in the body, according to what he has done, whether good or bad. Knowing, therefore, *the terror of the Lord*, we persuade men; but we are well known to God, and I also trust are well known in your consciences. (2 Cor. 5:9–11)

Here Paul is saying that his evangelism was in part motivated by his fear of God, by knowing who he would one day stand before. Where did he discover that? On the road to Damascus. The highly religious, highly zealous persecutor of the early church was on his way there to round up some more followers of Jesus when he was blinded by a bright light and fell to the ground.

When God asked Saul why he was persecuting Him, "he, trembling and astonished, said, 'Lord, what do You want me to do?'" (Acts 9:6). Paul had a frightening encounter with God that transformed him from chief persecutor to champion preacher. He met the One he had only thought he knew.

Paul had plenty of head knowledge about God and how holy He was—that was what had fueled his hatred of the church. He actually thought he was doing God a favor. Only when he encountered God as He truly is—in explosive, blinding brightness—did he realize how wrong he had been.

So dramatic was Paul's turnaround that he soon found himself on the wrong side of the Jewish leaders in Damascus. They plotted to kill him, but he managed to escape in time. Going to Jerusalem he continued to speak about Jesus, stirring others to try to kill him while he was there.

Yet the church continued to grow. "And walking in *the fear of the Lord* and in the comfort of the Holy Spirit, they were multiplied" (v. 31). I long to be part of a global church like that, don't you? Walking in the fear of the Lord, as they did at Pentecost, will get us there.

Let's Pray

Great King,

 I ask that You would do in me what You did in Your early believers.

 Lead me deeper, Lord, into fear, fire, and fellowship; and use me to turn the world upside down, amen.

CHAPTER 7

THE BIBLE IS FULL OF FEAR

That all the peoples of the earth may know
the hand of the LORD, that it is mighty, that
you may fear the LORD your God forever.
—JOSHUA 4:24

The more I've studied the fear of the Lord, the more I've realized that it's as much a part of the message of the Bible as God's great love for humankind; you can't really have one without the other.

As I read Scripture with new eyes, I begin to see this fearful aspect of God and His nature in so many familiar passages. It was like discovering a new side to someone. This can be uncomfortable, I know. Just how much so was brought home to me during a show For Today played in Atlanta.

We were at the Masquerade, an old brick building with wood floors that didn't seem to have been cleaned in a century or so, all feeling a bit like a castle. Candice and I decided that my two older boys were at an age to watch a show for the first time, from the wings of this famous venue.

There was a full house, several hundred kids getting into the music, and I was doing my thing, sweat and hair flying. Loud music. Strobe lights. Smoke. Energy. Aggression. To the uninitiated, pandemonium with a beat.

At one point I stole a glance to the side. Kai and Caleb were each clinging to one of their mom's legs, heads half-buried while peeking out at me with eyes wide like saucers, a mix of recognition and shock. It was as if they were saying, "This is Dad, but this isn't the dad we know." I went over to them during a song to give them a high five, to signal, "Hey, it's okay, it's me," but they weren't having any of it.

Only after the show did they come cautiously for hugs, as if to check it was still me, and I held them close as we went out front to talk and pray with people. This was their own Brock moment, when they discovered the fierceness of a father who was both their promise and their protection.

In a similar kind of way, I have found dimensions of God's fierceness and fearful nature in the stories of some well-known Bible characters.

ADAM

We don't have to wait long for fear to crop up in the Bible. It first appears in Genesis 3, after Adam and Eve did the one thing they were told not to do, eat from the Tree of Knowledge of Good and Evil.

God came for what seems to have been His regular walk with them in the garden and could not find them. When He called out,

Adam answered, "I heard Your voice in the garden, and I was afraid because I was naked; and I hid myself" (v. 10).

It's interesting that Adam and Eve weren't afraid of the Devil; they were afraid of being exposed before God. Even though they had only seen and known His goodness up to that point, that experience of pure, perfect intimacy with Him provoked fear at what breaking such communion would mean.

Yet we see so much of God's loving heart and kind intentions in this whole encounter. He didn't call out angrily, "How dare you!" or "You have betrayed me!" or "Get out of my sight!" Instead, He asked Adam, "Where are you?" (v. 9).

What an odd question. But as John Bevere points out in *The Fear of the Lord*, "Anytime God asks a question, He is not looking for information."[1] It's not as if God didn't know exactly where Adam and Eve were, after all. He asked the question because He was giving Adam room to respond, to move toward God in his sin. I suspect, too, that His tone was tender rather than stern, an invitation to come out of hiding rather than scaring him away. That God would show such tenderness to Adam even in his rebellion is a beautiful picture of His love for us all in our fallenness and brokenness. Yet God's question still evoked fear in Adam. He knew the enormity of what he had done.

What strikes me, too, is how God's main concern is revealed in His question in verse 11: "Who told you that you were naked?" He was not primarily focused on the fact that Adam had eaten from the banned tree—that question came second. First, above all, He was concerned that Adam and Eve had listened to the wrong voice.

In fact, that's the source, the essence of all sin, isn't it—*listening to the wrong voice*? As long as we are focused on God and what He has to say, we will be okay.

This is why it is so important that we pursue an intimate relationship with God, so that we can discern His voice from all the others clamoring for our attention. We can be confident that this is not only possible, but something God wants for us. Jesus said, "My sheep hear My voice, and I know them, and they follow Me" (John 10.27).

This story from the garden also should emphasize to us all just how seriously God views sin. Adam and Eve sinned only once, but that led to their separation from God and their banishment from His presence. Those were pretty serious consequences—for us all!

If only we viewed our own sin in the same way. Instead, we minimize and rationalize.

"It's just porn. It's not like I am actually having an affair."

"Did you hear about . . . ?"

"No one will notice it's missing."

While we see God's continuing love for Adam and Eve in Genesis 3, we also see the fearful, sobering consequences of their sin.

ABRAHAM

There is a pretty simple litmus test for knowing if someone fears God, and it's found in the Genesis 22 account of the life of Abraham, the father of our faith.

This episode is significant in a number of ways, including the fact that it is the first time the words *worship* and *love* are used in Scripture. But Abraham wasn't there on the mountain to sing songs or dance—he was there to sacrifice the thing he loved most in the world.

It was his son, Isaac, of course. This was the child Abraham and Sarah had waited for through many long years, born in their old age when it seemed impossible. If God was going to fulfill His long-ago promise to Abraham to make of him "a great nation" (Gen. 12:2), it would have to be through this son. Yet God told Abraham, "Take now your son, your only son Isaac, whom you love, and go to the land of Moriah, and offer him there as a burnt offering on one of the mountains of which I shall tell you" (22:2).

As a father myself, I can't imagine what went through Abraham's heart and mind, but he obeyed. He journeyed to the mountains of Moriah, built an altar, laid wood on it, then bound Isaac and laid him on top. Only at the last minute, as Abraham raised his knife, did God intervene. A voice came from heaven: "Do not lay your hand on the lad, or do anything to him; for now *I know that you fear God, since you have not withheld your son*, your only son, from Me" (v. 12).

Obedience. This was the measure of how Abraham feared God—that he did what God had directed even when it seemed to be counterproductive to the fulfillment of God's promise to him.

It's fairly easy to do what God says when you can understand what He's doing and even see the fruit of your actions. It is a whole lot harder when you don't understand, when what He is saying seems to move you away from the dream He's given you. Do we fear God enough to do what He says even when it's costly, inconvenient, or uncomfortable? We must realize that the real dream is intimacy with God, not productivity for God.

The fact is, He still wants us to be willing to "kill our babies" today. But, you say, God called you into ministry, and your church is flourishing. God gifted you in music and is opening so many doors for you. There's no way that He would want you to walk away from that and do something else.

Are you so certain? As it was for both Abraham and Adam, it comes down to hearing, honoring, and obeying God's voice and doing what He says, come what may. In Abraham's obedience, his unwavering trust, we also see how the fear of the Lord led to blessing. God had previously spoken to Abraham about birthing a people through him, but it was only after this encounter that He got specific. The angel of the Lord told Abraham:

DO WE FEAR GOD ENOUGH TO DO WHAT HE SAYS EVEN WHEN IT'S COSTLY, INCONVENIENT, OR UNCOMFORTABLE?

By Myself I have sworn, says the LORD, because you have done this thing, and have not withheld your son, your only son —blessing I will bless you, and multiplying I will multiply your descendants as the stars of the heaven and as the sand which is on the seashore; and your descendants shall possess the gate of their enemies. In your seed all the nations of the earth shall be blessed, because you have obeyed My voice. (vv. 16–18)

When people talk about "mountaintop" experiences in worship, they usually mean sweet moments when they are lost in a sense of God's love and peace. Abraham's mountaintop experience of worship was a far different thing. His fear of the Lord was evidenced by radical obedience.

JOSEPH

Many who point to Joseph as a great example of patient faith, someone who was ultimately rewarded for his enduring trust in God despite betrayals and setbacks, say his great faithfulness was fueled by his vision—that he never lost sight of the dreams he had as a young man.

I've no doubt that he did remember them during his "lost" years, but I don't think they were what kept him honest and humble throughout. I believe, rather, that he walked in integrity because he walked in the fear of the Lord.

Things had started to look up when Joseph arrived in Egypt with the Ishmaelites, who had bought him from his jealous brothers. He was purchased in turn by Potiphar, one of Pharaoh's officers, who quickly recognized Joseph's giftedness. He soon put him in charge of all of his affairs.

But then came trouble, in the seductive shape of Potiphar's wife. When she saw that he was a good-looking guy and offered herself to him, Joseph refused. One might have expected him to say something like, "Hey, thanks, but I couldn't betray my master like that after he has entrusted me with so much."

Read how he did answer, however: "Look, my master does not know what is with me in the house, and he has committed all that he has to my hand. There is no one greater in this house than I, nor has he kept back anything from me but you, because you are his wife. How then can I do this great wickedness, and sin against God?" (Gen. 39:8–9).

Joseph may have had good reason to fear Potiphar if word got out that he had been sleeping with his master's wife, but that wasn't what kept him out of her arms. It was his fear of sinning against God. He knew that he was only in the position he was in because God had put him there, and to disrespect that place would be to disrespect God.

Doing what God says may be the best measure of whether someone fears the Lord, but a close second is how that person fulfills his or her current obligations and commitments. I've met many people whose attitude is, "I believe God's going to use me one day, but right now I am only a [student, accountant, fill in the blank]."

With that kind of attitude, they approach today's responsibilities with less fire and integrity than they should, and then wonder why the future seems to be slow in coming. But just as we've been told, "God has a wonderful plan for your future," we must remember that He also has a wonderful plan for our present. We are where we are on purpose, and to despise our "right now" is to disqualify ourselves for our "what's next."

Whenever I think of Joseph's example, I am reminded of Jesus' parable of the unjust steward, who lost his job for poor performance. Jesus concluded the story this way: "He who is faithful in what is least is faithful also in much; and he who is unjust in what is least is unjust also in much. Therefore if you have not been faithful in the unrighteous mammon, who will commit to your trust the true riches? And if you have not been faithful in what is another man's, who will give you what is your own?" (Luke 16:10–12).

The fear of the Lord kept Joseph loyal and faithful through times of great trial.

JOSHUA

Without a proper fear of the Lord, there is a danger of getting too familiar in our faith. Yes, God is our loving heavenly Father and calls us into a life of intimacy with Him, but He is also still an all-consuming fire, in whose presence we only dare venture because of the protection of grace.

The Bible talks about people being "friends" of God, but I don't see any "buddies," as in the free-and-easy way I hear some people talk about Him. The bottom line is, He is God and we are not. Joshua got a good reminder of this as he prepared to lead the children of Israel into the promised land.

If someone might be expected to have a sense of the fear of the Lord, it was probably Joshua. As Moses' right-hand man, he'd been as close as anyone to him after his encounters with God on the mountain and in the Tent of Meeting. After Moses left the tent having met with God "face to face, as a man speaks to his friend" (Ex. 33:11), Joshua "would not depart from the tent" (NASB).

Still, he got a surprise when he went to check out Jericho, where he was met by "a Man . . . with His sword drawn in his hand" (Josh. 5:13). This could have been intimidating, but Joshua must have been feeling pretty confident. After all, God had spoken to him after Moses' death and told him that he was going to lead the people into the promised land: "Be strong and of good courage; do not be afraid, nor be dismayed, for the LORD your God is with you wherever you go" (Josh. 1:9).

With all that in mind, Joshua asked, "Are You for us or for our adversaries?" (Josh. 5:13). Like many, I believe that the way the "Man" is described here suggests that this was actually a preincarnate Jesus. His answer sent Joshua to his knees: "No, but as Commander of the army of the LORD I have now come" (v. 14). In other words, "I'm not on your side or your enemy's side. God has His own agenda here, and I have come to enforce it."

We read on: "And Joshua fell on his face to the earth and worshiped, and said to Him, 'What does my Lord say to His servant?' Then the Commander of the LORD's army said to Joshua, 'Take your sandal off your foot, for the place where you stand is holy.' And Joshua did so" (vv. 14–15).

This was not a time for casual appreciation and a "Hey, thanks for coming." The only right response in the face of such authority and power was to submit.

What I love so much about this encounter is how the fear of the Lord involved getting a correct perspective on what was going on. Yes, God was leading the people of Israel into the promised land, but He was not on their side. He reminded them that, actually, they were on His side—and that's the only safe place to be.

We need more of the same proper perspective in the church today. God doesn't choose sides between us and our enemies. God Himself has a side, and we and our enemies get to choose whether we are going to join it or not.

I've seen billboards put up by well-meaning churches that say things like, "God is for you." I appreciate the intent of the message, but I always think, *Well, He's for you unless He is against you!* The truth is, there are many people doing things and pushing agendas that God is most definitely against.

Now, He loves them, and He wants them to be free, but that's going to require them changing sides. God doesn't move; we do. I understand that this may sound harsh, but as my spiritual father has said many times, "If this is rubbing you the wrong way, maybe you need to turn around!"

True fear of the Lord will keep us from being presumptuous about our place in God's plans and purposes.

GIDEON

As I mentioned earlier, life isn't about having no fear at all; it's about being afraid of the right things. The fear of the Lord emboldens us to face things that previously scared us into passivity. Gideon is a great example.

For years the Israelites had been under the thumb of the Midianites, who would plunder Israel's crops and livestock. They would swoop down, snatch up what they wanted, and then ride off, leaving the Israelites with almost nothing. God's chosen people were "greatly impoverished" (Judg. 6:6).

That was why Gideon was threshing wheat in a sheltered wine-press when the angel of the Lord appeared to him. This is not the best way to thresh wheat. You're supposed to do it in an open space, throwing the wheat up into the air so the wind can blow away the chaff (seed casings and other debris).

But Gideon was scared of being seen by the Midianites, so he preferred to settle for the inferior bread that would result from threshing in a confined space. In the light of that, being greeted as a "mighty man of valor" (v. 12) seems almost laughable, but it was actually prophetic. God knew that in hiding was a man waiting to be released to be a hero.

Gideon wasn't impressed by his visitor. In fact, he gave him a little attitude. Maybe all those years of frustration finally boiled up. If God was with him, he wanted to know, why were things so bad? Why didn't he see the power of God he had been told about? Then, in Judges 6:14, we read, "Then the LORD turned to him and said, 'Go in this might of yours, and you shall save Israel from the hand of the Midianites. Have I not sent you?'"

Hoping for some sort of confirmation, Gideon scrambled to bring an offering. He prepared a goat, some broth, and some unleavened bread and set them down before the visitor, "and fire rose out of the rock and consumed the meat and the unleavened bread. And the Angel of the Lord departed out of his sight" (v. 21).

Only then did Gideon fully realize to whom he was talking: "Gideon perceived that He was the Angel of the Lord. So Gideon said, 'Alas, O LORD GOD! For I have seen the Angel of the LORD face to face'" (v. 22).

Gideon was terrified, recognizing that he was in the presence of almighty Yahweh: "Then the LORD said to him, 'Peace be with you; do not fear, you shall not die'" (v. 23).

After that encounter, Gideon found the strength to step out of hiding. It was a gradual journey for him, for sure. His first task—to pull down his family's idolatrous Asherah poles (wooden images)—he did at night so he wouldn't be seen. But he grew in faith and stature—to the point that the man who once hid in a winepress whittled down an army from twenty-two thousand to three hundred, and then took them into battle armed only with a torch and a trumpet.

Part of what fueled Gideon's faith, I believe, is that he knew that if God truly was with him, then nothing was impossible. When first visited by the angel of the Lord, Gideon had asked, "O my lord, if the LORD is with us, why then has all this happened to us? And where are all His miracles which our fathers told us about, saying, 'Did not the LORD bring us up from Egypt?'" (v. 13).

God's reply in the next verse is significant: "Then the LORD turned to him and said, 'Go in this might of yours, and you shall save Israel from the hand of the Midianites. Have I not sent you?'"

Gideon's might, his source of strength, was the knowledge that "if God is with me, then things are going to change; things are going to be different."

I believe that today God is looking for believers who will use "God is with us" not as a morale booster but as a standard setter. Yahweh is searching, even now, for the "might of Gideon" again—men and women who, despite their weakness, will stand up and say, "If God is really with us, where are the miracles our fathers experienced?" It is that righteous indignation that moves His heart and invites His hand into our lives in a profound and inescapable way.

Wouldn't you like the same sense of anticipation and expectation that Gideon had? If God is with you, isn't it time to come out of hiding? Shouldn't things look different in your life, in your family, in the lives of those around you?

That is the strength that God will use to change the course of history, as a healthy fear of Him inspires courage. He did it in Gideon's time, and He will do it again in ours!

JEHOSHAPHAT

As we will get into later in the book, the fear of the Lord isn't just a mystical experience we get to talk about with others and that makes us seem really spiritual. It's an intensely physical thing, in the sense that it should affect the way we live from day to day: where we go, what we do, what we say.

King Jehoshaphat knew that.

A righteous king of Judah, Jehoshaphat "walked in the former ways of his father David; he did not seek the Baals, but sought the God of his father, and walked in His commandments." He "took delight in the ways of the LORD" and tore down the idolatrous high places in his kingdom. Through his strong stand, "the fear of the LORD fell on all the kingdoms of the lands that were around Judah," and with profound results: "They did not make war against Jehoshaphat" (2 Chron. 17:3–4, 6, 10).

Later in his reign, Jehoshaphat went out on a sort of mini revival tour among some of the people and "brought them back to the LORD God of their fathers" (19:4). He then appointed judges in the cities and instructed them how to perform their duties: "Take heed to what you are doing, for you do not judge for man but for the LORD, who is with you in the judgment. Now therefore, *let the fear of the LORD be upon you*; take care and do it, for there is no iniquity with the LORD our God, no partiality, nor taking of bribes" (vv. 6–7).

Jehoshaphat gave the same instruction to the Levites, priests, and heads of families he appointed to handle matters in Jerusalem: "Thus you shall act in the fear of the LORD, faithfully and with a loyal heart . . . Do this, and you will not be guilty . . . Behave courageously, and the LORD will be with the good" (vv. 9–11).

We certainly need to heed Jehoshaphat's instructions today. We live in a culture that screams, "Don't judge! Don't judge!"—although, contradictory as it is, many want to be free to make their own judgments about things. They just don't want others to be free to disagree with them. People even quote Jesus—"Do not judge, or you too will be judged" (Matt. 7:1 NIV)—as evidence that we shouldn't evaluate other people and their actions.

But that's taking His words seriously out of context. Paul wrote, "But he who is spiritual judges all things" (1 Cor. 2:15). And besides, after warning that we who judge will also be judged, Jesus Himself went right on to say, "For with what judgment you judge [others], you will be judged; and with the measure you use, it will be measured back to you" (Matt. 7:2). His point being that the yardstick we use to measure others will be used on us.

Only in the fear of the Lord will we be able to judge things well. If more of us walked in Jehoshaphat's counsel today in the way we handled disagreements and disputes, it would make a big difference.

I think we'd start by cleaning up a whole lot of the lies and nonsense of the carnal world that have so deeply woven themselves into the collective value system of the modern church.

DAVID AND UZZAH

There are several lessons on the fear of the Lord that we could draw from the life of David, but let me focus on just two here. First, like Gideon's, David's fear of the Lord positioned him to overcome any other fear and lead others against God's enemies.

The Israelite army had been camped out against the Philistines for some time when David arrived with provisions for his older brothers. There must have been some capable fighters in the Israelite ranks, but not a single man was willing to step forward and take on Goliath, the Philistines' champion. This guy was a monster: his chain mail coat weighed more than 120 pounds. That would be like me going out to fight someone with a small adult on my back. His spear weighed about as much as a large bowling ball.

Yet David didn't think twice before offering to go and take him on. Why? Because he told King Saul that Yahweh, "who delivered me from the paw of the lion and from the paw of the bear, He will deliver me from the hand of this Philistine" (1 Sam. 17:37). He wasn't referring to some distant deity or ancient idol; he was talking about "the living God" (vv. 26, 36).

When Goliath tried to trash-talk David into backing down by ridiculing his small frame and lack of armor and weapons, David answered fiercely, "This day the LORD will deliver you into my hand, and I will strike you and take your head from you. And this day I will give the carcasses of the camp of the Philistines to the birds of the air and the wild beasts of the earth, that all the earth may know that there is a God in Israel" (v. 46).

The God whom David was talking about here isn't nice and easy-going; He's wild, violent, and scary.

This is such a great reminder to us all. Yes, our God is the caring Shepherd of whom David wrote (Psalm 23), and the kind and loving Lord he praised (117:2; 145:17), but He is also the great Warrior King who is with us, and our enemies had better watch out!

We all know that David's life has other important examples to offer. The man after God's own heart not only became an adulterer but he also arranged Uriah's death to cover up his unfaithfulness with Bathsheba, Uriah's wife (Acts 13:22; 2 Samuel 11). He also made the mistake that can trip up all of those who press in hard to God—he got careless.

Everyone was celebrating when David went to bring the ark of the covenant back to its rightful place in Jerusalem. People were singing and dancing as the procession made its way to Nachon's property, when the oxen pulling the cart onto which the ark had been loaded stumbled.

Second Samuel 6 picks up the story: "Uzzah put out his hand to the ark of God and took hold of it, for the oxen stumbled. Then the anger of the LORD was aroused against Uzzah, and God struck him there for his error; and he died there by the ark of God" (vv. 6–7). The New International Version calls Uzzah's error an "irreverence"—an act that revealed a lack of fear of the Lord, a failure to honor His holiness, a carelessness to God's commands.

At first glance, God's response might seem unreasonably harsh. Uzzah had only tried to save the ark from falling—and was struck dead for it. But we need to understand the backstory. When God first spoke to Moses about the ark of the covenant, He gave specific, explicit instructions (Exodus 25). Specifically, the ark was to be fitted with four gold rings, through which two gold-covered poles could be inserted, and it was to be carried by the priests.

Instead, it had been thrown on the back of a cart.

But God's presence is not to be treated lightly, and David learned that. Second Samuel 6:9 says that after witnessing Uzzah's death, "David was afraid of the Lord that day."

Uzzah's death wasn't just about doing things differently. The people had failed to hallow God's name, to recognize Him as holy in their actions. They became careless, just as Aaron's sons did.

David learned his lesson, though. When he later returned to bring the ark home, the cart seems to have been pushed to one side. Instead, we read of "those who bore the ark" (2 Sam. 6:13 esv). And with a renewed sense of fear and wonder, "David danced before the Lord with all his might" (v. 14).

Let's Pray

Holy One,
You have been faithful and fierce throughout all time.
I tremble as I see You now for who You really are. Forgive me
for the times I have ignored this side of Your character, and mark
me now as one, like David, who is after Your heart, amen.

CHAPTER 8

THEN AND NOW: THE FEAR OF THE LORD ENDURES

The fear of the LORD fell on the people,
and they came out with one consent.

—I SAMUEL 11:7

The first time I was ever invited somewhere to speak, I stepped out on the stage naked. Not literally, of course, but in every other sense of the word. The message I had spent weeks preparing on a series of index cards lay discarded at the side of the platform, where I had left them. I had no notes, no Bible, no clue what I was going to say, nothing but the sense that God had told me to step out and trust Him.

This was not what I'd had in mind. I'd preached between songs at a lot of For Today shows before, but this was the first occasion I'd been asked to show up as a speaker, not a performer. I'd been excited about the opportunity and also conscious of not wanting to let down the pastor who had asked me, so I had prayed and studied hard.

My audience was a crowd of teenagers at a big hotel in Phoenix, Arizona, where their parents were gathered for a denomination's international conference. Some of them knew me from my musical career, so I was expecting a warm reception. I was pretty pumped as I waited to be introduced, and then God whispered, *Do you want to do this, or do you want Me to do this?*

I put down my Bible and notes, walked out empty-handed, and gave what may go down as one of the shortest messages ever. With my fairly recent trailer encounter with God and a recent reading of Moses' burning bush experience fresh in my mind, I told the teen audience that I didn't really have anything to give them—that honestly, I didn't have anything to give anyone. The fruit of my life and ministry had been God's work, not mine, and the best I had ever done by way of ministry was to get out of the way so He could be the center of attention.

Pointing to a line on the carpet in front of the stage, I asked everyone to step back behind it—then invited anyone who wanted more of God to cross it. "If you want an encounter with God today," I said, "I want you to step across this line. But before you come, take off your shoes, because I hear God saying, 'This is holy ground.'"

No one moved for what felt like forever, just a sea of young faces looking at me blankly, like "Where's the sermon?" Then one kid moved. A chubby little guy, about fourteen, slipped off his shoes and came forward. As soon as he stepped over the line on the ground his whole body began to shake, and he hit the floor, sobbing hard into the carpet.

Several kids took a few steps back in alarm, but then one or two others came forward too. The same thing happened to them. Within a few minutes there were dozens of teenagers kneeling or lying down, weeping in the presence of God. Then His power began to spread throughout the room as many began to shake and fall to their knees right where they were.

A girl who'd damaged her ankle dancing during the earlier concert was waiting at the back of the room for paramedics to come and take her to the nearest ER. She asked someone to carry her forward, and when they crossed the line, she was instantly healed. All around, tears were turning to shouts of joy; it was amazing.

I noticed one girl moving closer, but she didn't seem convicted like the others. More like curious, even questioning. When she stepped over the line, she also fell down, but this time it was different. She began to writhe and growl, her hands twisted up and her face contorted.

I knew what was happening, but I was way out of my depth. The darkness that had afflicted her in secret had suddenly come into the brilliant light of Christ, and it couldn't hide anymore. I went over to her, praying, "God, You said You wanted to do this, and You're going to have to. Please come and do it."

A couple of the leaders who had invited me to the event joined me, and we prayed for her as she thrashed and fought and cursed and made threats. After just a few moments, one of the other guys touched her on the forehead, and said, "Peace. Be still, in Jesus' name." With that, she calmed down immediately and seemed to go into a restful sleep.

And so it went on, kids falling down under conviction and rising in new wonder and thankfulness for God's grace and mercy, some being set free from demonic oppression. It was nothing like I had planned, but more than I could have hoped for. The problem was, these were all pastors' kids.

Not everyone was happy about it. Some parents were concerned when word started to leak out about what had happened. There was even a meeting about it all the next day, when some of the denominational leaders wanted to know how and why this young guy with tattoos and no ministry credentials had been let loose on their kids. I wasn't there, but someone told me later that the president of the denomination had heard everyone's concerns and questions, then gently told them that if God was moving, he would never question who He chose to move through.

That episode in Phoenix continues to mark the way I do ministry. I'm not cavalier or offhand about what I have been called to do. When I am invited somewhere, I will pray ahead of time and do some preparation, but whenever I step out to speak, I always listen for God's leading, rather than relying on my strategies or methods. I am ready to lay aside what I've readied for what I hear from Him.

My time with those young people also made me realize that what I'd experienced previously, in Virginia, wasn't unique. I'd already begun to discover the fear of the Lord running through Scripture like a vein of unmined gold, but as I started to talk to others and read and research, I found that the fear of the Lord had continued beyond the Bible and throughout the pages of church history.

It seems that whenever God is moving in purifying power, a new awareness of and appreciation for the fear of the Lord is inescapably present. I could probably fill a whole book with examples, but here are just a few.

"INFINITELY PURE AND HOLY" IN AMERICA

Anyone who knows anything about how God has moved mightily in America in the past has heard about the First Great Awakening, which touched thousands of people, and has probably heard the name Jonathan Edwards as well.

He was the man who preached the famously titled sermon "Sinners in the Hands of an Angry God," which reportedly had people crying out for God's mercy and clinging to the posts in churches for fear that they might fall into hell. A contemporary printing of the message he delivered to a church in Enfield, Connecticut, in July 1741, stated that it was "attended with remarkable impressions on many of the hearers."[1] The language is old-fashioned, but it means they were fearful!

WHENEVER GOD IS MOVING IN PURIFYING POWER, A NEW AWARENESS OF AND APPRECIATION FOR THE FEAR OF THE LORD IS INESCAPABLY PRESENT.

Curious to find out more, I read a copy of Edwards's historic message and came away a bit surprised. It was certainly plain speaking, and he didn't pull any punches about the measure of God's wrath for those outside His love and mercy, but I didn't see anything in there that seemed to be that remarkable.

The impact of that sermon wasn't due to Edwards's great eloquence. In fact, it seems he wasn't a notable speaker. According to an early biography, when he was in the pulpit, "his words often discovered a great degree of inward fervor, without much noise or external emotion . . . He made but little motion of his head or hands in the desk, but spake as if to discover the motion of his own heart, which tended in the most natural and effectual manner to move and affect others."[2]

He didn't even have a good sound system to fall back on so he could emphasize his points with a shout or a stage whisper. There was no praise band playing quietly in the background to create a kind of emotive atmosphere, nor any mood lighting. Just his pure passion for God, rooted in what his biographer called Edwards's "deep abiding sense of divine things on his mind, and of his living constantly in the fear of God."[3]

The result: almost three hundred years later, his message remains one of the best-known sermons in history. Though he is perhaps best remembered for having preached "Sinners" at the church in Enfield, he had shared the same message and others—he used to write his sermons out ahead of time, then read them—previously, also with powerful results.

In an account of the revival that occurred in Northampton, where he pastored between 1740 and 1742, he wrote of an occasion when many were "exceedingly overcome; and the room was filled with cries; and when they were dismissed, they almost all of them went home crying aloud through the streets, to all parts of the town."[4] Another time, "many others . . . were overcome with distress about their sinful and miserable estate and condition; so that the whole room was full of nothing but outcries, faintings, and the like."[5]

Edwards remembered:

It was a very frequent thing to see a house full of out-cries, faintings, convulsions, and such like, both with distress, and also with admiration and joy. It was not the manner here to hold meetings all night, as in some places, nor was it common to continue them till very late in the night; but it was pretty often so, that there were some that were so affected, and their bodies so overcome, that they could not go home, but were obliged to stay all night where they were.[6]

All this wasn't just an experience that passed away. All those living in Northampton who had been touched during the revival were invited to make a covenant with God to live more fully for Him. Among the things they pledged:

And furthermore we promise, that we will strictly avoid all freedoms and familiarities in company, so tending, either to stir up, or gratify a lust of lasciviousness, that we cannot in our consciences think will be approved by the infinitely pure and holy eye of God, or that we can think, on serious and impartial consideration, we should be afraid to practice, if we expected in a few hours to appear before that holy God, to give an account of ourselves to him, as fearing they would be condemned by him as unlawful and impure.[7]

The fear of the Lord inspired them to live holy lives.

"A HUNGER AND A THIRST" IN SCOTLAND

In 1949 Duncan Campbell arrived in the Hebridean islands—a wind-swept grouping off the rugged northwest coast of Scotland, in the Atlantic Ocean—at the invitation of two elderly sisters who for a long time had been praying for revival in their community. What happened next, centered on a move prompted by the fear of the Lord, is still spoken of widely as a powerful work of God.

Though he had been traveling all day from Edinburgh, Campbell was invited to preach at an evening meeting when he arrived. After speaking to around three hundred people in the local church, it was almost 11:00 p.m. when he left—only to find twice that number waiting for him outside the building.

Around a hundred young people had been at a dance at the local parish hall, who "weren't thinking of God or eternity," Campbell recalled later. "They were there to have a good night when suddenly the power of God fell upon the dance. The music ceased and in a matter of minutes, the hall was empty. They fled from the hall as a man fleeing from a plague. And they made for the church."[8]

Meanwhile, men and women who had gone to bed got up, dressed, and also headed for the church. "A hunger and a thirst gripped the people," Campbell said of the six hundred people standing outside. Faced with the crowd, he and his hosts turned back and opened the doors of the church. Making his way through the crowd to the pulpit, he passed a young woman, a teacher at the local school, lying prostrate on the floor and crying out, "Oh, God, is there mercy for me? Oh, God, is there mercy for me?"⁹

The second service finally finished at about 4:00 a.m., though without any kind of altar call. "You never need to make an appeal or an altar call in revival," Campbell said. "Why, the roadside becomes an altar. We just leave men and women to make their way to God themselves."¹⁰ Finally leaving the church, Campbell and his hosts were approached by a young man who asked him to go to the police station.

"What's wrong?" Campbell asked.

"Oh, there's nothing wrong," the man said, "but there must be at least 400 people gathered around the police station just now." As at the church, people had somehow felt compelled to go there—some coming from more than twelve miles away in a coach. Campbell described the scene:

> The people are crying to God for mercy. Oh, the confessions that were made! There was one old man crying out, "Oh, God, hell is too good for me! Hell is too good for me!" This is Holy Ghost conviction! Now mind you, that was on the very first night of a mighty demonstration that shook the island.¹¹

And so it went on, during a season that saw conviction and conversions sweep across the islands.

Another time Campbell was summoned to preach at 3:00 a.m. at a church where hundreds had gathered. "The Spirit of God was moving, oh, moving in a mighty way," he said. "I could see them falling, falling on their knees. I could hear them crying to God for mercy. I could hear those outside praying."¹²

Meanwhile, many more who could not get into the church had gathered in a nearby field. "I saw this enormous crowd standing there as though gripped by a power that they could not explain," Campbell said.[13]

One night, a man living fifteen miles away, on the mainland, "suddenly was gripped by the fear of God." When he told his wife he had to go out right away, she thought it was an excuse to go drinking. Finding someone to ferry him across the water, he reached a farmhouse where Campbell was preaching at around midnight, "and in a matter of minutes he was praising God for salvation."[14]

Looking back on those experiences some years later, Campbell warned of the danger of "allowing ourselves to drift in an easy current of conventional Christianity and conventional mission-work." He went on, "Somehow, we have lost the sense of urgency because we have lost the subduing sense of God—that sense of God that a past generation spoke of as 'the fear of God.' I know of no greater tragedy than to lose the sense of the immediate presence of God."[15]

What we've been referring to as "the fear of the Lord," Campbell called "the sense of the immediate presence of God." I like that. That's what it is, after all—as in my life-changing encounter in the Virginia Beach prayer room, it's the simple acknowledgment of and adjustment to the knowledge that "God is here."

"SOBS AND CRIES" IN BRAZIL

In *The Fear of the Lord*, John Bevere wrote of a time when he was in Brazil and he became distressed by the casual attitude in a meeting at which he had been invited to speak. While the worship was enthusiastic, he noted "a complete absence of the Lord's presence."[16] Though he had been in other meetings where people had showed a lack of respect, it had never been to this degree, he recalled, sensing that God wanted him to confront what was happening:

I was determined to say nothing until I had their attention. I felt godly indignation burning within my breast. After a minute, everyone fell silent, realizing nothing was happening on the platform.

I did not introduce myself or greet the crowd. Instead I opened with this question, "How would you like it if, while you spoke with someone, they ignored you the entire time or continued to carry on a conversation with the person next to them? Or if their eyes roamed with disinterest and disrespect?" . . .

Then I stated firmly, "Do you think the King of kings and Lord of lords is going to come into a place where He is not given due honor and reverence? Do you think the Master of all creation is going to speak when His Word is not respected enough to be listened to attentively?"[17]

When John went on to preach, the atmosphere changed. At the close of his message, he invited anyone who had been convicted of their irreverent attitude to stand. Most people did, and John prayed for them. "Immediately the presence of the Lord filled that auditorium," he wrote. "Although I had not led the congregation in a prayer, I heard sobs and cries rising from the crowd. It was as if a wave of God's presence had swept through the building, bringing cleansing and refreshing . . . I watched as people wiped away tears."[18]

The moment subsided, but soon John sensed another wave of God's presence.

The only way I know how to describe it is to compare it to standing a hundred or so yards away from the end of a runway as a huge jet takes off right in front you. This describes the roar of the wind that immediately blew through that auditorium. Almost simultaneously the people erupted in fervent and intense prayer, their voices rising and combining into almost a single shout.

When I first heard the rushing wind, I reasoned that a jet had just flown over the building. In no way did I want to attribute something to God if there was a chance that it was not. My mind raced to remember the proximity of the airport. It was nowhere nearby, and two hours had passed with no sounds of planes overhead.

I turned inward to the Spirit, realizing I could sense the presence of God in an awesome way and that the people had exploded into prayer. This was certainly not in response to an airplane's passing overhead.[19]

Later John learned that security personnel and police officers on duty outside the building—where it was "just another calm Brazilian evening"—had reported a roaring noise coming from inside.[20]

"RIVERS OF TEARS" IN SOUTH AFRICA

I first heard another remarkable account from Joy Dawson, whose book *Intimate Friendship with God* helped me grow in my understanding, as did John Bevere's.

Speaking at a church in California,[21] she read a report of what happened when missionaries arranged a screening of the evangelistic *Jesus* movie at a refugee camp in South Africa filled with thousands who had fled the fighting in neighboring Mozambique. Many women and children there had lost husbands, fathers, and sons in the violence. Conditions in the camp were terrible: water was scarce, and relief workers struggled to provide people with one small meal a day. According to an official report I obtained later from Cru (formerly Campus Crusade for Christ), which runs the movie outreach, "the smell of human excrement overpowered the senses almost as heavily as the cloud of hopelessness and spiritual darkness."

In this setting a small team set up to show the movie, even though it wasn't available in the Shangaan language spoken by the refugees. They decided to screen the English version and have an interpreter translate as it played.

Joy read how, as the film crew were setting up the screen, they could hear witch doctors chanting and saw them throwing bones on the ground as they called up the spirits of their ancestors. That prompted the film team to call for some concentrated prayer and intercession before the screening for around a thousand refugees. Joy shared a firsthand report from one of the teams of what happened toward the end of the movie:

> Everyone suddenly started to cry: women, men and children. A mournful wailing gradually rose from the crowd into a relentless crescendo. As Jesus was being pushed down the Via Dolorosa, in the film, the weeping became louder and totally uncontrollable. When the Roman soldiers started nailing Jesus to the cross, many of the people jumped up and ran towards the screen with their hands in the air, crying out to God. Everywhere people were confessing their sins. The film was forgotten, rivers of tears poured down their dirty cheeks . . . Some were on their knees, some stood with their eyes closed and arms raised, others lay prostrate on the ground . . . These people were in the presence of a holy God. They were overwhelmed by a sense of their sinfulness and wanted desperately to be forgiven.[22]

The team leader recalled:

> I felt the awesome power of God, I felt his love, his compassion, his care. It was overpowering. It was a wave that welled up inside us and we couldn't contain it. We were totally, irrevocably, hopelessly in love with Jesus . . . I saw a nine-year-old boy crying out to God,

I turned to pray for him but I couldn't because I was crying too much myself. A seventy-year-old man with his eyes open and his hands in the air repeated over and over again, "I just saw Jesus, I just saw Jesus." . . .

Another member of the team said,

I knew I was in a holy place. These people have nothing . . . not even enough water, and God decided to give them a chance right there in that filthy camp to feel His presence and His overwhelming love.[23]

Eventually things calmed down enough that the team was able to continue the showing. When it came to the part about Jesus' burial, the interpreter explained how Jesus died for our sins and was raised from the dead, at which point the "the crowd exploded as if a dam had burst, everyone began cheering and dancing, hugging one another and jumping up and down."

The team never even finished the screening. An invitation was given to those who wanted to receive Christ to come to the front, and everyone responded.

AND IT'S STILL HAPPENING

Though some of these stories happened many years ago, they continue to stir me and others when I recount them because I believe God continues to reveal some of His glory through them, inviting us to want to experience the same thing.

I remember how this happened once when I was meeting at my home with a friend, who works with me in ministry, and his brother, who was not walking with God. This brother told me that he believed in God in an abstract kind of way, but he'd never had any kind of personal experience with Him.

I didn't preach to him at all. Instead, I just started telling stories of some of the times I'd encountered God and how they had marked me. As I spoke, tears began to roll down the young man's cheeks.

Then we became aware of a sound, like a rushing wind filling the small prayer room in my house. It seemed to roll up from downstairs into the second-floor room where we were sitting. Neither my friend nor I prayed for his brother or said anything directly to him, but I looked over and saw him suddenly lying prostrate on the floor, shaking and sobbing into the carpet as God's mighty presence filled the room.

Stories of how God has touched others can create a hunger in us for the same kind of touch. If we do not hunger, we will never be filled.

Let's Pray

Lord,

Thank You for the many times and ways You have revealed Yourself to us.

I ask that You would move again in our generation in a way that is beyond explanation or description.

Send Your spirit of revival and awakening upon our land, and turn our world upside down, amen.

CHAPTER 9

THE THRONE ROOM

*Let Your ear be attentive to the prayer of
Your servant, and to the prayer of Your
servants who desire to fear Your name.*

—NEHEMIAH 1:11

When Dorothy, the Scarecrow, the Tin Man, and the Cowardly Lion finally got their audience with the ruler of the Land of Oz, flames burst into the air, and a voice boomed out, "Do not arouse the wrath of the great and powerful Oz!"

Dorothy and her friends quaked in fear, but then Dorothy's little dog, Toto, tugged at a curtain in the corner of the ruler's audience room and pulled it to one side. Behind it was not the fierce, formidable figure of people's imaginations, but a little old man pulling levers.

Sad to say, but I believe this climactic scene in the famous movie version of Frank L. Baum's classic *The Wizard of Oz* is played out every Sunday in too many churches—but in reverse.

Using gadgets and special effects, some churches present God as a kindly, well-meaning grandfather, while keeping people from experiencing the full magnitude and awe-inducing intensity of His true nature. Rather than make Him seem more than He really is, they make Him seem less than He really is!

In the movie, once his fakery was revealed, Oscar Diggs, the small man pretending to be the fearsome wizard, roared through his microphone, "Pay no attention to that man behind the curtain." But it was too late; his fraud had been exposed.

I believe that as Christians, we need to do the exact opposite: we *need* to look beyond the facade religion has built and focus more of our attention on what is behind the veil, as it were, in God's throne room.

Thankfully, we are able to do that because of what Christ did at Calvary.

There was a time when only the high priest could enter into the Holy of Holies, the place where God was most present, and then only once a year, on the Day of Atonement.

Even then, it was at great risk. According to Jewish tradition, the high priest would tie a rope around his waist so that his body could be pulled from the inner sanctum should he forget the protocol that God's presence demanded and die for the mistake. But when Jesus became our ultimate High Priest (Heb. 4:14), He ended that separation.

We don't have to wait until a special day once a year anymore for someone else to approach God on our behalf. We have free access ourselves. Because of Jesus' sacrifice, "we have boldness and access with confidence through faith in Him" (Eph. 3:12).

At the very moment Jesus gave up His spirit on the cross, "the veil of the temple was torn in two from top to bottom" (Matt. 27:51). The consequences of this are so important, yet so little understood.

You see, we often talk about "the presence of God" as though it comes and goes. What we should recognize is that our awareness or experience of the presence of God—or His glory, as the Bible often calls it—may come and go.

I used to seek to encourage people to hunger for a day when they would have free and constant access to God by telling them the promise of Habakkuk 2:14, that "the glory of the LORD" will cover the earth "as the waters cover the sea." Then I reread the Scriptures more carefully and found what this verse actually says: "For the earth will be filled with *the knowledge* of the glory of the LORD, as the waters cover the sea."

It doesn't promise that the glory will fill the earth one day, sometime in the future. Instead, it says that the knowledge of God's glory will cover the earth. Because of Jesus' death and resurrection, we are all constantly surrounded by the glory of the Lord. He is not far from me, or you, at all (Acts 17:27). We just may not be aware of it.

Take a moment to consider the tremendous declaration made by one of the seraphim the prophet Isaiah saw flying around the throne of God: "Holy, holy, holy is the LORD of hosts; the whole earth is full of His glory!" (Isa. 6:3). Did you catch that? I read that passage for years, and thought to myself, *Surely the angel meant that all of* heaven *is full of His glory. Surely he meant that the whole* throne room *is full of His glory.* But no. The Word of God clearly declares that the whole earth—the place we live—is full (to capacity) of God's glory!

To experience that reality, we may need to change the way we think about the glory of God. How many of our favorite songs beg God for something that surrounds us already? How often do we pray, "God, send Your glory!" We, like Eve in the garden, when the tempter convinced her she needed to eat fruit to become like God, are constantly being tempted to earn something we've already been given.

Remember, Eve had already been made like God. God said, "Let Us make man in Our image, according to Our likeness" (Gen. 1:26).

Then, we read, "God created man in His own image; in the image of God He created him; male and female He created them" (v. 27).

We are like Him and we are near Him! And now we must be willing to finally step into the place of intimacy with God that was once hidden behind the veil. That will mean being open to encountering and understanding Him in ways that we may not have so far. He is a loving Father, but He is also a scary God.

THE APOSTLE WHO FEARED HIS FRIEND

If anyone knew Jesus well when He was on earth, it was the apostle John. He seems to have held a special place in Jesus' heart, referring to himself in his gospel as "the one Jesus loved" (John 20:2 NIV). We know, too, that at the Last Supper John got to sit in the favored spot next to Jesus, because he was the one who was "leaning back on Jesus' breast" (John 13:25).

WE MUST BE WILLING TO FINALLY STEP INTO THE PLACE OF INTIMACY WITH GOD THAT WAS ONCE HIDDEN BEHIND THE VEIL.

You might say that John knew Jesus' heartbeat well! He shared it through his gospel, telling of God's great love. He wrote one of the most-quoted verses in the Bible: "For God so loved the world that He gave His only begotten Son, that whoever believes in Him should not perish but have everlasting life" (3:16).

Later, in his letter to the early church, John wrote, "Behold what manner of love the Father has bestowed on us, that we should be called children of God!" and "Beloved, let us love one another, for love is of God," and "God is love" (1 John 3:1; 4:7, 16).

Clearly, John knew God to be loving and good and kind. But fast-forward with me toward the end of the apostle's life, when he was exiled on the Mediterranean island of Patmos, where he would write his Revelation. While he was in prayer, John had an amazing encounter with Jesus—the One he had known intimately—at which he "fell at His feet as dead" (Rev. 1:17).

What was so terrifying that it caused him to collapse like that? Having heard a loud voice tell him to write down in a book what he saw, John recalled:

> And having turned I saw seven golden lampstands, and in the midst of the seven lampstands One like the Son of Man, clothed with a garment down to the feet and girded about the chest with a golden band. His head and hair were white like wool, as white as snow, and His eyes like a flame of fire; His feet were like fine brass, as if refined in a furnace, and His voice as the sound of many waters; He had in His right hand seven stars, out of His mouth went a sharp two-edged sword, and His countenance was like the sun shining in its strength. (vv. 12–16)

That sounds overwhelming enough, but there's more. After John was invited to "come up here" and was then drawn up into heaven (4:1), he recounted:

> And He who sat there was like a jasper and a sardius stone in appearance; and there was a rainbow around the throne, in appearance like an emerald. Around the throne were twenty-four thrones, and on the thrones I saw twenty-four elders sitting, clothed in white robes; and they had crowns of gold on their heads. And from the throne proceeded lightnings, thunderings, and voices. Seven lamps of fire were burning before the throne, which are the seven Spirits of God. Before the throne there was a sea of glass, like crystal. And in the midst of the throne, and around the throne, were four living creatures full of eyes in front and in back. The first living creature was like a lion, the second living creature like a calf, the third living

creature had a face like a man, and the fourth living creature was like a flying eagle. The four living creatures, each having six wings, were full of eyes around and within. And they do not rest day or night, saying: "Holy, holy, holy, Lord God Almighty, Who was and is and is to come!" Whenever the living creatures give glory and honor and thanks to Him who sits on the throne, who lives forever and ever, the twenty-four elders fall down before Him who sits on the throne and worship Him who lives forever and ever, and cast their crowns before the throne, saying: "You are worthy, O Lord, to receive glory and honor and power; for You created all things, and by Your will they exist and were created." (Rev. 4:3–11)

You may be familiar with this passage, so take a moment to slow down and take in the scene. Try to put yourself in John's shoes and see what he saw. Eyes piercing and flickering like flames of fire as they searched and exposed the deepest parts of his being. A countenance like the brightest sun. Shining stones. Lightning, thunder, and the rumble of voices roaring like waves from the throne. Burning lamps of fire. The dark clouds and smoke curling in the air around the flapping of the wings of those great creatures before a massive throne, and the whole room shaking under his feet.

Special effects in movies have desensitized us a bit to real life. We see explosions and earthquakes courtesy of CGI (computer-generated imagery) and think, *How cool!* instead of *How scary!* Think back, though, to the last time you may have made an open fire. Can you feel that fierce heat in your face from just a few logs? Multiply that a thousandfold or more to have a sense of what John experienced. No wonder he fell on his face.

This is Jesus as the untamed Lion of Judah, not the neutered and declawed house cat some churches have turned Him into. And this is not the heaven many of us have in mind. There are no fluffy clouds or chubby little angels quietly playing lutes.

I've heard some people say that the prospect of heaven seems kind of boring, but that's certainly not the case by this account!

This scene that shook John in his sandals is also a long way from what many of us think of when we think about church. It is God on what used to be the other side of the veil. And while that veil has been torn down, many of us choose to live as though it's still there. We'd prefer not to venture in that close ourselves. We'd rather have someone go there and report back for us with a to-do list, like the Israelites did:

> Now all the people witnessed the thunderings, the lightning flashes, the sound of the trumpet, and the mountain smoking; and when the people saw it, they trembled and stood afar off. Then they said to Moses, "You speak with us, and we will hear; but let not God speak with us, lest we die." (Ex. 20:18–19)

NO COURTESY CLAPS IN HEAVEN

Revelation is the last book in the Bible, of course, and so it's not the first time we see people who knew God well—and whom He knew as faithful servants—experience a new, scary dimension of Him. Nine hundred years before John was overwhelmed by the mighty presence of God, the prophet Isaiah was also given a glimpse of what heaven—and the God of heaven—is really like. "In the year that King Uzziah died," he wrote, "I saw the Lord sitting on a throne, high and lifted up, and the train of His robe filled the temple" (Isa. 6:1).

Isaiah's reaction? "Woe is me, for I am undone!" (v. 5). In other words, *Oh no! I'm a dead man.*

Again, what did Isaiah see that prompted such a reaction? He wrote that above the temple "stood seraphim":

Each one had six wings: with two he covered his face, with two he covered his feet, and with two he flew. And one cried to another and said: "Holy, holy, holy is the LORD of hosts; the whole earth is full of His glory!" And the posts of the door were shaken by the voice of him who cried out, and the house was filled with smoke. (vv. 2–4)

We know, too, that there were flames, for one of the seraphim—whose name means "burning ones" in Hebrew—flew to Isaiah with "a live coal which he had taken with the tongs from the altar" to purge the prophet's lips (vv. 6–7).

This is another familiar passage where we may lose the intensity of what happened. The place was filled with smoke. The foundations of the thresholds were shaking. No wonder Isaiah was in fear.

The phrase "the LORD of hosts" (v. 3) is a translation of the Hebrew *Yahweh Sabaoth*, where *Sabaoth* means "an innumerable throng or limitless company." This is the God of heaven's enormous army, with Him as its commander in chief. He is not receiving a courtesy clap from the angelic beings in this passage! It is all they can do to cry out, "Holy, holy, holy" (v. 3). *Holy* means to be set apart, different—they simply have to acknowledge how more, how other, how unique He is. There is no one, nothing, like Him.

Isaiah's subsequent strength to do what God told him to do came from his experience with a scary God. Having encountered God in His fierce holiness, he wanted to serve Him: "Here am I! Send me," he cried (v. 8).

But first there had to be that encounter with the fire of God: "Then one of the seraphim flew to me, having in his hand a live coal which he had taken with the tongs from the altar. And he touched my mouth with it, and said: 'Behold, this has touched your lips; your iniquity is taken away, and your sin purged'" (vv. 6–7).

Though Isaiah had prophesied for five chapters before this encounter, he still cried out, "I am a man of unclean lips" (v. 5). He had already spoken on behalf of God. He had already been preaching, leading, and directing the spiritual lives of the nation of Israel, but now he was ashamed of the uncleanness of his lips, as his eyes finally beheld the Holy One he'd spoken so much about. It was only after this vision that Isaiah could go with confidence, conviction, or clarity. He would no longer speak on behalf of a God he'd heard about, but a God he'd seen. He would never again be one going for God, but one going from God.

It's worth noting that Isaiah said yes before he even knew the details of his assignment. Only after he had stepped forward did God then tell him where to go and what to say—and the message he was given was not exactly a popular one (vv. 9–10). Yet Isaiah delivered it because he knew how fierce and mighty was the One who had given it to him.

The prophet Ezekiel also got his marching orders after experiencing the glory of the Lord. He wrote of creatures "like burning coals of fire, like the appearance of torches going back and forth among the living creatures. The fire was bright, and out of the fire went lightning. And the living creatures ran back and forth, in appearance like a flash of lightning" (Ezek. 1:13–14).

Then he saw "the likeness of a throne, in appearance like a sapphire stone; on the likeness of the throne was a likeness with the appearance of a man high above it. Also from the appearance of His waist and upward I saw, as it were, the color of amber with the appearance of fire all around within it; and from the appearance of His waist and downward I saw, as it were, the appearance of fire with brightness all around" (vv. 26–27).

The fiery, fierce God that John, Isaiah, and Ezekiel encountered is not an anomaly. Years ago, a friend of mine was praying and worshiping with his four-year-old son before bed one night, when the boy suddenly looked up and said to him, "Daddy, the orange Man loves me." This little boy had caught a glimpse of the burning God, the One the fathers of our faith described as looking like a jasper or sardius stone, or amber; an "orange Man" at once so full of love that little children come freely and joyfully before Him, and yet so horrifying that demons tremble at the mention of His name.

That little boy didn't experience anything different from those who wrote biblical accounts. All of them experienced the overwhelming intensity of our unchanging God. Centuries apart, they got to know something more of the One who dwells "in unapproachable light" (1 Tim. 6:16).

So did Daniel, another faithful servant, who told of what he saw: "I watched till thrones were put in place, and the Ancient of Days was seated; His garment was white as snow, and the hair of His head was like pure wool. His throne was a fiery flame, its wheels a burning fire; a fiery stream issued and came forth from before Him" (Dan. 7:9–10).

Once again, consuming fire. Not surprisingly, Daniel was alarmed: "I . . . was grieved in my spirit within my body, and the visions of my head troubled me" (v. 15). In fact, he was so scared that the blood drained from his face: "My thoughts greatly troubled me, and my countenance changed" (v. 28).

When Daniel, Isaiah, and John entered the throne room of God, they beheld indescribable, otherworldly things that made their hearts pound and drove them to their faces. These were men who already loved and honored God, who walked in His ways as best they knew how—but when they encountered more of Him, they were undone.

I wonder what Sunday church service might look like if we arrived with an anticipation of that same sort of encounter. As I've said, we don't go to church to find God's presence because it's not kept separate from us as it used to be in the Old Testament. The veil has been torn in two.

At the same time, we do gather as church members to *worship* God. God is "holy, enthroned in the praises of Israel" (Ps. 22:3). So, in a very real way, our church gatherings can become an extension of God's throne room.

Sadly, they are often more like shopping malls.

THE ONLY RIGHT RESPONSE

The tendency of some churches to be too casual, too familiar in worship was uncomfortably illustrated for me in a dream I had while working on this book.

In my dream I was visiting a museum with some of my friends. When we get together we can be kind of loud sometimes. We're full of enthusiasm and energy, and we come at life as if it's supposed to be lived to the full. We don't want to miss out on anything.

That's how we were when went into this museum, a really fancy building full of magnificent works of art. We wanted to try to take everything in while we were there: we were running around, pointing things out to each other, taking photos, just having a great time. We were boisterous in the presence of beauty, enjoying all that we were seeing.

When we'd finished touring this incredible vault of art treasures, we walked down the street and came to a small, nondescript building. The name outside said it was the museum of atomic weaponry, or something like that. Because admission was free, we decided to go in and have a look around. There wasn't much to see—just one live atomic bomb on display in the center of the main room, separated from visitors by only a rope.

Suddenly my friends and I became very, very respectful. I noticed that we walked slowly and carefully, speaking in hushed voices, aware that we were in the presence of an incredible, awe-inspiring power. We knew that one false move could mean destruction.

There is a place for exuberant, joyful praise and worship in our churches, of course. I think it will be richer and deeper and purer and sweeter, however, when it is grounded more in heaven, if you will, fueled by a greater sense of what we have to be thankful for, what we have been saved from, and what we've been saved for—knowing the fearful reality of who Yahweh truly is.

This is not something that can be manufactured by creating the right atmosphere. It's all God, and when it happens, it doesn't need controlling.

One of the first times I spoke about what I have learned about the fear of the Lord over the past few years was in a church in São Paulo, Brazil, in early 2017. I had preached there previously, and this time I felt God telling me to speak about this message that had been growing inside me for the past few years.

It didn't take long. I was still in the early stages of my studies, so I didn't have a whole lot to say. I simply spoke from Exodus 3, about Moses' encounter with God in the burning bush and how he met a God who was more than he had ever been taught or believed.

"At the end of the day, it will not be my great preaching or the great worship songs that set you free from your sin and that burn away every flawed thing in you," I said. "It will be God. Just seek His face; encounter Him; pursue Him."

Then it started, from the back of the room into which around four hundred people were crammed. They began to fall, some into their seats, some down onto their knees, some flat on their faces. It was like watching the wind blow over a cornfield, bending the stalks in waves. Some people wept; some were silent. No one sent any text messages.

I fell to my face on the stage, pressed down as I had been in that trailer in Virginia. It felt as if the floor were vibrating. I didn't look up, but I sensed deep in me that God was meeting His people all around the room, healing, freeing, delivering. Someone would cry out, confessing sin. Another would weep.

After a while, part of me thought, *Okay, Mattie, you've got to wrap this all up somehow.* I thought I should finish things up nicely, maybe pray a blessing, and send everyone home.

But then quickly came a correction from the Holy Spirit: *Don't do anything. Don't touch this.* I was fearful to put my hand to something God had in His. After a while I got up quietly, stepped back off the stage, and left, not waiting to pray for people afterward or to chat and sell books. For all I know, they could still all be there on the floor!

When God is on the throne—in His rightful place of honor—you're not needed. And when God moves, there is only one appropriate response in that moment: sheer, awestruck, worshipful wonder.

Let's Pray

Yahweh,

You are holy! You are incomparable and indescribable; glorious in majesty and beyond imagination!

I see You, and though I do not need another glimpse to convince me of Your worthiness, I long to see You more!

You transcend all human greatness and overwhelm my faculties. No words suffice. You are holy, amen.

CHAPTER 10

GOD'S KINDNESS AND SEVERITY

You who fear the LORD, praise Him!
All you descendants of Jacob, glorify Him,
And fear Him, all you offspring of Israel!
—PSALM 22:23

Let's take a hike together. We're going to climb this mountain that rises into the distance. It's beautiful as we make our way up the trail. There are trees and flowers as we rise, rocks and streams we step over. The air is fresh and clear, and we can hear the birds calling. We see deer running, hear other wildlife rustling in the bushes. Our hearts beat a little harder as we gain altitude, and the views get better the farther we can see. It's simply delightful; we pause to sit and soak it all in, just a short way from the summit.

But now scramble with me to the very top. As we get closer, we can feel heat growing. There's a smoky tinge to the air. Cresting the peak, we look over and down—into a huge volcano. The lava glows red deep below, waves of heat rising from deep inside the earth. Anything, anyone that fell in there would simply be consumed. Vaporized.

None of this detracts from what we have seen on the way up or makes it any less beautiful. But we've realized there is more going on here than we were aware of, and that we need to tread lightly. The beautiful views of the mountain don't exist without what is on the other side. This is something of the true nature of God. He is not either-or. He is both-and.

That is why Paul could write urging the early church to "consider the *goodness and severity* of God" (Rom. 11:22). He did not see the two in opposition to each other, but more like the twin blades of a pair of scissors—the cutting edge is where they come together. With that image in mind, it's appropriate that the Greek word translated as "severity" is *apotomia*, which means "roughness, rigor, sharpness, a cutting off."

Paul went on in the same verse to refer to the severity of God "on those who fell . . . but toward you, goodness, if you continue in His goodness." We should want to do everything we can to avoid God's severity; Hebrews 10:31 warns that "it is a fearful thing to fall into the hands of the living God."

How have we come to emphasize the kindness of God over—and sometimes to the exclusion of—His severity, in so many of our churches? At least a couple of reasons spring to mind—one having to do with Christians, and the other relating to those who don't know Jesus.

First, many of us in the church want comfort more than we want commitment, if we're honest with ourselves. We want all the good things that can come from knowing God without having to sacrifice too much. If you think I'm being too harsh, just look around the next time your church service runs a little long and see how many people are checking their watches or their phones and starting to getting irritated. They seem more concerned about their convenience than about what God may want to do or say.

Second, we've decided that we need to soft-pedal things a bit to make God more palatable to the lost. So we preach how loving and merciful and accepting He is without mentioning His severity because we don't want to put them off.

I agree with John Bevere when he says that this overemphasis is "not real grace, but a perversion of it. This is the result of overemphasizing the *goodness* of God to the neglect of the *fear* of Him."[1]

Real grace actually requires fearing God: "Therefore, since we are receiving a kingdom which cannot be shaken, let us have grace, by which we may serve God acceptably with reverence and *godly fear*" (Heb. 12:28). Yet God has always sent messengers to warn people of the danger they were in if they did not turn from their ways— from Jeremiah and Isaiah and Jonah, among the prophets, to Peter and Paul.

In much of the church today, we've basically decided that we can improve on God's original idea. We're doing things for Him without Him. We may be very devout; we may "read our Bibles daily, and attend every prayer meeting," John Bevere observes. "We can preach great and motivating sermons, work hard in the ministry for years, and even receive the respect and admiration of our peers. But if we do not fear God, we are only climbing the rungs of the religious ladder."[2]

Some churches are even presenting themselves as "safe spaces." I think I get what they are trying to communicate in these days when we are more sensitive to how people may come with deep hurts and wounds, but for me it communicates an inaccurate truth regarding what really happens in God's presence. Church is a place of rescue and restoration, but not a place of relaxation.

If church is a place committed to the pursuit of God, then it should be far from safe, maybe even the least-safe space, because throughout Scripture people felt anything but safe in His presence. It's where we find out that everything we thought we knew about ourselves and life was wrong, and where we get to repent, die to ourselves, and pick up our crosses and follow Christ.

We cannot really know God's loving-kindness without knowing His severity. Only when we understand just what we have been saved from will we really have a deep awareness of God's love and then be moved to love Him in return. Jesus observed that "to whom little is forgiven, the same loves little" (Luke 7:47).

From my experience of sharing the gospel with people, just telling them how much God loves them isn't enough, no matter how sensitive it sounds. They don't just need to know that there is a God who loves them and forgives them. They also need to know that there is a God who will go to war with whatever keeps them in fear and bondage. A God who is stronger than what is oppressing them. A God who is fiercer than the demons that are harassing them. A God who is mightier than the addiction that is gripping them. A God who is greater than the wounds and weaknesses that are holding them back.

The reality of fallen man is that he is utterly lost, surrounded by an enemy called Self that will choke the life out of him without mercy. He is outgunned and helpless if God will not fight for him. But the moment he recognizes his hopeless condition and calls to the cross for rescue, Yahweh will rise from His throne and go to war on his behalf. And when Yahweh goes to war, no enemy stands a chance!

TO WORSHIP GOD PROPERLY, WE MUST SEE HIM CLEARLY

When we lose sight of God's severity, we stop seeing His kindness clearly too. These two sides of the coin of God's character are inescapably linked, and we cannot neglect the truth of His severity and embrace the idea of His kindness without losing the reality of both. I believe that our view of His love then becomes distorted, with serious consequences.

One result is that we become too familiar with God. As I have said before, He is not our "buddy." Yes, we can become friends with God, but there are conditions. He is not just friendly to everyone. As John Bevere has written, "In the Scriptures, the only people I see God calling His friends are those who tremble at His Word and presence and are quick to obey, no matter the cost."[3]

Jesus said, "You are My friends *if you do whatever I command you*" (John 15:14). That is not blanket buddyhood.

Perhaps most worryingly, our worship becomes distorted when we abandon any recognition of God's severity. Because we focus so much on God's love for us, we measure the richness or quality or depth of our worship by how it makes us feel. We often talk about the songs we like to sing. But what about stopping to wonder which songs God likes for us to sing?

By basing worship all on our emotions, we have cheapened it. In fact, I'd go as far as to say that in some ways we have turned it into spiritual pornography. Does that offend you? Well, I don't mean to come off as judgmental, but I believe that God is offended by some of what passes for worship in many modern churches. Often we have turned what was intended to be a corporate act into a corporate event organized to entertain those in attendance.

It's part of a wider mistake we have made in the church, trading Christian instruction for Christian entertainment. Instead of feeding people meat, we have been serving them candy.

Worship has become a spectator sport, where we watch a singer or a band perform for us, and we may or may not join in. The emphasis is on sounding good to people rather than sounding good to God. People are chosen for the worship team for their talent and fashion sense rather than their passion for God. Some churches pay session musicians who aren't even members to come and play.

I remember one time preaching in a church that had been struggling for some time. It wasn't growing, and the people there were tired and discouraged. I discovered that while the worship leader was a godly woman, someone she'd let be part of the worship team was not only living in a way that clearly violated God's teaching but was openly denying God's existence. He got to play, though, because he was good at his instrument.

The worship leader may have thought she was being inclusive, but she had created an atmosphere in which production was more important than pursuit, and in such an atmosphere, worship will never be more than a performance. I am convinced that if God could not trust them to maintain the integrity of their leadership team, He would certainly not trust them with influence or impact in their city.

This kind of performance mentality means that the church has a lot of rock stars but few fathers—lots of people to look up to when they are onstage, but not necessarily when they are offstage.

It has also reduced a lot of our music to cheap imitations of other people's ideas. Instead of being at the forefront of creativity, which we should be as people filled with the Spirit of the One through whom all things were created, we follow what the world is doing. We rip off the latest hit band, redoing their riffs and producing a sanitized, "family-friendly" "Christian" version.

Okay, you might be thinking, *tough but not entirely unfair. But spiritual pornography? That's going a bit far.*

Let me explain. I believe that we live in a culture that has been so polluted sexually that we don't realize that porn has shaped the way we view so many other things. When it comes to spirituality, many times our approach is just the same as with sexuality. We would prefer to see intimacy than engage in it ourselves. We watch others to have our desires satisfied, at least superficially.

Porn makes no demands. It requires no responsibility. You have no obligation to that naked person on the screen. You don't have to be vulnerable with him or her; you don't need to risk exposing yourself. You don't have to say you're sorry when you make mistakes, or help pay the bills and raise the kids.

It can be the same with much of our contemporary worship. You don't have to pay the price of covenantal pursuit required to have intimacy with God; you can just watch others. No investment, no requirement.

But God is pretty clear, when it comes to physical relationships, that we are not to be intimate with another person without a covenant. So why would we expect to be able to be intimate with God without a covenant? Like our spouses, He wants to know we have forsaken all others and all other things. God isn't into the "friends with benefits," casual hookup thing. Why should we think we can party hard on Saturday night and praise well on Sunday morning?

Porn reduces the incredible richness of sexual intimacy as God intended it to be to a mere act. What was meant to be three-dimensional becomes two-dimensional, flat. Similarly, spiritual porn reduces what God intended for worship—to be a multifaceted expression—to one thing, performing. That is so far from what it should really be about. True worship is a lifestyle of pursuit, not a genre of music.

WHY WOULD WE EXPECT TO BE ABLE TO BE INTIMATE WITH GOD WITHOUT A COVENANT?

If regular porn makes someone an adulterer, spiritual porn makes him or her an adulator whose attention has turned toward the people making the music, not toward the One for whom music should be made. God takes this very seriously: the first of the Ten Commandments is "You shall have no other gods before Me" (Ex. 20:3).

I was reminded how important this is a few years ago when we were in Memphis to play a For Today show at a church that had organized it as an outreach. We got a pretty good reception from the moment we hit the stage: the kids in the front were really into it, with their arms raised and their eyes closed. But something felt off to me.

I was trying to work out what was wrong as we played, and then God whispered something to my spirit: *They're worshiping you, not Me. You're in the way tonight.*

It was like a punch in the gut. I turned to the other guys and gave them the neck-slashing sign to stop playing. Quickly I told them what I'd heard and that God had said we should just play worship music for the rest of our set. They nodded their agreement as I turned back to the audience.

"I heard God say while we were playing that you've been worshiping us, not Him, and He is offended by idolatry," I said. "I don't ever want to be the idol that God is offended with, so let's turn our attention to Him and just see what He'll do."

One challenge was that we knew only one worship song. So we just played it repeatedly for the remainder of our set while I prayed for people and spoke prophetic words. It worked. Obedience always works. I sensed a shift in the direction of people's hearts, away from us and toward God, and He responded. People were touched.

TRUE WORSHIP

A few years ago, my oldest son, Kai, asked me, "Daddy, what is worship?" I reflected for a moment before offering an answer I thought a five-year-old could understand, an answer to a question I'm not sure I'd ever adequately understood myself.

"Worship is anything you do to show God that you love Him," I said.

What's key about this is that it becomes about you, not someone else you look to, like a song leader. Worship is no longer twenty minutes of singing before the Sunday sermon. It might involve you using your voice to tell God how you love Him and how grateful you are to Him, but it may not. It may be helping clean up the church kitchen after an event, or pushing your kids on a swing, or taking your spouse on a date, or telling the girl at the grocery store checkout that God sees her and loves her.

In doing those things, we're showing God that we are thankful for the church family He has made us part of, for the children He has blessed us with, for the life partners He has entrusted to us, for the opportunity to tell someone else about His grace and mercy and goodness. And we don't need to wait for someone else to lead us into that.

The emotion-centered way many churches approach worship these days has created an unhealthy dependency among believers. If the music isn't great, if the atmosphere isn't cool, people don't feel they have encountered God. But mature believers shouldn't need anyone else to carry them into His presence. We should be able to go to Him on our own.

Jesus taught that the kingdom of heaven is like ten virgins who took their lamps and went out to meet the bridegroom. When he arrived in the middle of the night, the five virgins who had brought oil lit their lamps and were ready, but the five who had not brought any oil ran out. They asked the five forward thinkers to share some of their oil. The story unfolded:

But the wise answered, saying, "No, lest there should not be enough for us and you; but go rather to those who sell, and buy for yourselves." And while they went to buy, the bridegroom came, and those who were ready went in with him to the wedding; and the door was shut.

Afterward the other virgins came also, saying, "Lord, Lord,

open to us!" But he answered and said, "Assuredly, I say to you, I do not know you." (Matt. 25:9–12)

Remember that this is a picture of the church: all ten women were virgins. There weren't five good girls and five good-time girls. All were faithful. All were waiting for the bridegroom. But five were reliant on others to keep their flames burning, while the others had the capacity within themselves to fuel their flames.

I get concerned when I see Christians who go from conference to conference and from church to church looking for the latest buzz. My fear is that they end up living off someone else's oil, whether that's the pastor or the speaker or the worship leader. They need to have their own source, so that if they don't have a Christian event to go to or a Christian book to read or a Christian TV show to watch, they know they can go to God on their own.

When we walk in the fear of the Lord, we won't need someone else to call us to worship; we'll want to run there ourselves. If you've ever truly seen Him for who He is—both kind and severe—no one will ever need to beg you to worship Him again.

Let's Pray

Lord God,

I see now that Your severity is in equal proportion to Your kindness.

You are both just and merciful; righteous and compassionate.

I choose today to worship You for who You really are, as I consider the boundless scope of Your godhood, amen.

CHAPTER 11

FEAR AND DELIGHT

Afterward the children of Israel shall return and seek the LORD *their God and David their king. They shall fear the* LORD *and His goodness in the latter days.*

—HOSEA 3:5

The meeting was set for a coffee shop. I'd agreed on a public space so there'd be witnesses to what went down, in case the other guy tried to spin things later to get me into trouble. As a backup, I also had a friend sit out in the parking lot and observe so he could offer a version of what happened, too, if needed.

I was there to do some straight talking with a casual acquaintance of Candice and mine who'd made a big mistake. He'd sent my wife some flirtatious, sexual text messages that had upset her and ticked me off big-time.

I'm not sure what he expected when I came in. He knew I was

a Christian, so maybe he thought I was going to have a gentle heart-to-heart, invite him to come to church, and sing "Amazing Grace" with him. But I wasn't there for any Jesus-meek-and-mild thing. I let him have it in no uncertain terms. Though I am generally a pretty easygoing, laid-back kind of guy, I'm big enough to be intimidating when I need to be.

I wasn't out of control when I went in to where he was sitting. I was used to being in intensely confrontational situations from my years with For Today. I knew exactly what I wanted to say and how I wanted to say it. But I'd planned ahead that he might just get the idea I was about to lose it.

So I made a bit of a scene. Without repeating here what I said, I made it abundantly clear through my words, my tone, and my body language that he had made a very—*very*—big mistake, and that it might be wise for him to avoid me and my wife from now on—like, walk the other way if he ever saw me coming down the street.

This wasn't about preserving my pride. It was about zeal for my marriage, protecting my wife's purity and honor. I knew God could have mercy for this guy, but my job right then as a husband was to go to war against that which threatened my bride. And I did. This man was left with no doubt that he had crossed a boundary, and he'd be wise not to even think about doing it again.

As aggressive and off-putting as they may have been, I believe my actions that day were God's mercy in the offender's life. I suspect he saw the seriousness of his secret sin for the first time that afternoon. He was invited to consider the damage he was trying to cause and the justice that he was in danger of experiencing.

When I got back to my truck where Candice was waiting, she whispered a quiet, "Thank you." Later she told me that even though she'd seen me in attack mode at shows many times, she had been a little unnerved by my intensity in that coffee shop.

There's a time to get angry. Failure to embrace this is one reason the church is so weak. We end up ignoring or accepting things that we shouldn't because we think it's wrong to ever get aggressive. I've even heard preachers say that God's not angry.

I'm not sure what Bible they're referencing. Mine is full of examples of God's anger. Do a word search and you will find plenty of times God is angry. For example: "God is a just judge, and God is angry with the wicked every day" (Ps. 7:11). No, the issue is not whether God gets angry, but why and with what and with whom.

God is angry at everything that mars His creation. He is angry at everything that threatens those He loves, that comes against them— not because He is hateful, but because He is moved to war against the things that oppose the object of His affection. Just as I was in that coffee shop.

God is angry that corrupt politicians keep people impoverished. He is angry that selfish businesspeople charge exorbitant prices for medicines. God is angry that thousands of children around the world die each day because of dirty water. He is also angry that violent men abuse women and children. God is angry that self-absorbed pastors stand in His spotlight to line their pockets

THE ISSUE IS NOT WHETHER GOD GETS ANGRY, BUT WHY AND WITH WHAT AND WITH WHOM.

and inflate their egos, while those they've been called to shepherd are starving, physically and spiritually. There's a lot that God is angry about.

This anger stems from His great love for us—a great cosmic force that relentlessly consumes every noneternal thing in its path. His love is jealous (Ex. 34:14); it is passionate and unrelenting. To be the object of God's love is to be the trophy for which He steps into battle. His hatred toward compromise, injustice, or deception is the other edge of the sword of His love.

One powerful example of God's anger can be found in 2 Samuel 22. It's the song David wrote thanking God for saving him from his enemies and from Saul, a version of which also appears in Psalm 18.

I've referenced this before, but let's look again at Psalm 18:7–18, seeing what happens when you threaten those God loves:

Then the earth shook and trembled;
The foundations of the hills also quaked and were shaken,
Because He was angry.
Smoke went up from His nostrils,
And devouring fire from His mouth;
Coals were kindled by it.
He bowed the heavens also, and came down
With darkness under His feet.
And He rode upon a cherub, and flew;
He flew upon the wings of the wind.
He made darkness His secret place;
His canopy around Him was dark waters
And thick clouds of the skies.
From the brightness before Him,
His thick clouds passed with hailstones and coals of fire.

The LORD thundered from heaven,
And the Most High uttered His voice,
Hailstones and coals of fire.
He sent out His arrows and scattered the foe,
Lightnings in abundance, and He vanquished them.
Then the channels of the sea were seen,
The foundations of the world were uncovered
At Your rebuke, O LORD,
At the blast of the breath of Your nostrils.

He sent from above, He took me;
He drew me out of many waters.
He delivered me from my strong enemy,

> *From those who hated me,*
> *For they were too strong for me*
> *They confronted me in the day of my calamity,*
> *But the LORD was my support.*

This isn't like someone sitting down to have a calm chat about something he doesn't like and asking the other person to maybe consider changing their ways, please. This is someone reacting strongly to an offense and coming to draw a line in the sand in no uncertain terms.

God was so indignant that smoke came from His nostrils and fire from His mouth, like a dragon. Things around Him appeared to spontaneously combust because of the intense heat that emanated from Him.

His voice thundered as He swooped down on a rescue mission. He flung out arrows and lightning bolts, laying bare the earth. He plucked David to safety, snatching him from the jaws of death.

Why? Not because He needed David. The king apparently knew that. He wrote that God "delivered me *because He delighted in me*" (2 Sam. 22:20).

God's delight in David wasn't blind. He knew David was a worshiper, a warrior—and an adulterer and a murderer; some say he was also a rapist.

David did not himself kill Uriah the Hittite, Bathsheba's husband, after she became pregnant with his child, but he arranged for the man's death. Trying to cover up his sin, David had Uriah called back from the war that was going on and attempted to set him up so he could hide his guilt.

But Uriah was too loyal to his fighting brothers to get some R & R while they were still out in the field—a stand that must have further pricked David's conscience. Desperate to cover his tracks, David then sent Uriah back to the battlefront, giving orders to the commander

Joab: "Set Uriah in the forefront of the hottest battle, and retreat from him, that he may be struck down and die" (11:15).

This was a cowardly move to cover up a previous sin that sometimes gets downplayed. David slept with Bathsheba after spotting her bathing as he walked on his roof and arranging for her to be brought to him; we all know the story.

Yet, like me, you may read this account in a slightly different light, in the wake of the recent #MeToo movement. The text isn't explicit, but it is certainly possible that this wasn't an entirely consensual relationship, bad enough as that would have been. It wasn't a sweet romance. If David didn't actually rape Bathsheba, then he almost certainly used the imbalance of their relationship—he was the king, after all—to get his way.

I think it's important to refresh our memories about all of this backstory, because this is the man in whom God delighted, and for whom He arose in anger. David was not perfect—far from it. He had not "earned" God's concern. But he was, despite all his failings, still a man after God's heart (Acts 13:22).

God's delight had nothing to do with any inherent quality that David had. David himself knew that. He wrote, "Every one of [the children of men] has turned aside; they have together become corrupt; there is none who does good, no, not one" (Ps. 53:3).

God's delight in David speaks to His inherent creativity, like an artist who paints a picture so beautiful that he falls in love with it. In humans, God created something that moves His heart and draws His affection.

THE COST AND REWARD OF GOD'S DELIGHT

I catch a glimpse of God's heart for us in my heart for my three boys. They do not have to do anything to cause my delight; they awaken it in me just by their very existence. I love everything about them—every movement of their hands, every expression on their faces. It's not what they do but who they are—mine—that makes me delight in them.

And, as with my wife, I am angered by anything that would come against them to try to diminish them—whether that's from outside or from within. If they are threatened by something external, I will step in to protect and rescue them.

When I see things like pride or self-centeredness or greed in them, I will also step in. I am angered because I know these things are enemies of God's best for my boys. I will go to war against them—not against my sons personally. Because I delight in my children, I will not settle for less than they should and can be. That's how God is with us.

God's delight isn't just emotion; it's also action. He doesn't just feel good things toward us; He brings good things to us. When God delights in us, He hears our cries for help. He is moved to come down to bring us out of bondage.

When God spoke to Moses from the burning bush, He told him, "I have surely seen the oppression of My people who are in Egypt, and have heard their cry because of their taskmasters, for I know their sorrows" (Ex. 3:7). The result is revealed in the next verse: "So I have come down to deliver them out of the hand of the Egyptians, and to bring them up from that land to a good and large land, to a land flowing with milk and honey" (v. 8).

Caleb and Joshua knew that God's delight could make the seemingly impossible possible. While the other ten spies who went to check out the promised land for Moses were overwhelmed by the giants they saw there, Caleb and Joshua were confident that God could help them prevail against their enemies.

They told the people,

The land we passed through to spy out is an exceedingly good land. If the LORD delights in us, then He will bring us into this land and give it to us, "a land which flows with milk and honey." Only do not rebel against the LORD, nor fear the people of the land, for they are our bread; their protection has departed from them, and the LORD is with us. Do not fear them. (Num. 14:7–9)

There is nothing you can ever do to earn God's delight. Going to church more regularly won't do it. Memorizing more Bible verses won't do it. Getting a handle on that besetting sin won't do it. You cannot produce God's delight in you—but you can better position yourself to receive and experience it.

We do that by hiding ourselves in Christ, by jumping into that underground bunker of my firestorm dream, which I shared in chapter 1. With a wall of flame racing toward you across the land, you'd be crazy to think, *Well, I'd better pull up some weeds around here so I deserve to get into the shelter.* No, you just run for safety!

Then, when we are safe, the fire comes and burns away all that has choked and stifled the land, and we can emerge to begin to sow and tend and harvest.

Remember that, according to Isaiah 11:3, which is speaking prophetically about Jesus, "His delight is in the fear of the LORD." Where He sees the fear of the Lord, Jesus is delighted. So as we embrace and walk in the fear of the Lord, we find ourselves in the scope of God's delight.

For many, this idea will require a real shift in their understanding of what God is like. It is essential that we have a right view of God, though. A. W. Tozer said, "What comes into our minds when we think about God is the most important thing about us,"[1] and that is so true.

SEEING THE CROSS THROUGH A VIEW-MASTER

The way we view God will shape our understanding and experience of Him. The smoke-snorting, fire-breathing, lightning bolt–hurling God portrayed by David in the previous section is far from the picture many Christians have of Him.

For some He's just a sad old man with a long beard, sitting in heaven, begging for a bit of attention. This isn't a God who can defeat our enemies and deliver us from our bondages. Nor is He a God who commands the attention of those who don't know Him. After all, if He can't do much for those of us who do know Him, why should anybody else listen to what we say He could do for them?

For some He's a loving Father, or a praiseworthy Redeemer, or a miraculous Healer. They know and have experienced some dimensions of His nature. But He is so much more than any of these individual aspects.

Before any of them, He is the Ultimate. He is the One who answers to no one, the One who sits enthroned above every other power, every other voice, every opinion. He is God, the great I Am, beyond the highest height of our imagination and the farthest breadth of our comprehension. He exists beyond the capacity of all human vocabulary and artistic expression. He is beyond speculation or criticism. He is Yahweh Elohim, the Father of Lights, in whom there is no change or shadow of turning (James 1:17).

He may be fatherly toward me, but He's not just Father. He may be friendly with me, but He's not just Friend. He may have saved me, but He's not just Savior. He is God without limit.

When Moses was told to return to Egypt and bring the Israelites out of slavery, he kind of asked God for His credentials: "When I come unto the children of Israel, and shall say unto them, The God of your fathers hath sent me unto you; and they shall say to me, What is his name? what shall I say unto them?" (Ex. 3:13 KJV).

God's answer, in the next verse, was succinct: "I Am." Me. Yahweh. The previously, presently, eternally existent One. End of story.

Before virtual reality goggles ever hit the market, there was View-Master, the red plastic stereoscope toy in which you placed a circular reel of pictures. Each scene had two identical images that, when viewed at the same time through both eyes, created a 3-D effect. Only by looking at both views simultaneously did you get the full effect.

It's the same sort of thing with God. Only when we see His love and His anger together, overlaid, as it were, do we get a true picture.

That is also the case when it comes to the cross. Some preachers and writers have painted the cross as a picture of God's mercy, but it is not only that. It's also a picture of God's justice.

Sin had to be dealt with. If God were only merciful, He could have simply ignored our sin. If He were only just, He could have called us to account for it. But He is just and merciful—taking our place under the weight of the wrath our sin deserved and positioning Himself to take every last drop of the cup of it upon and into Himself.

A SCANDALOUS TRUTH

Unfortunately, the way some preachers talk about the crucifixion, they actually water down the depth of what happened. I've heard some say how much it must have broken God the Father's heart to see Jesus hanging on the cross. "But He did it for you," they say as they play the pity strings, so you feel bad for God and almost end up responding to the altar call as a favor to Him.

That's not the way it went. A prophetic passage from Isaiah 53 explains:

He was oppressed and He was afflicted, yet He opened not His mouth;
He was led as a lamb to the slaughter, and as a sheep before its shearers

is silent, so He opened not His mouth. He was taken from prison and from judgment, and who will declare His generation? For He was cut off from the land of the living; for the transgressions of My people He was stricken. And they made His grave with the wicked—but with the rich at His death, because He had done no violence, nor was any deceit in His mouth. Yet *it pleased the* LORD *to bruise Him.* (vv. 7–10)

Some translations use the word *crush* rather than *bruise*, which adds to the severity of what took place. But did you catch the other really important part of that last verse, that it "pleased the LORD to bruise Him"?

This sounds scandalous, offensive, almost heretical. How could such a thing be true of a God who is love—not just loving, but love itself?

Yet Scripture says God was pleased to do this. Not just prepared or willing, but *pleased. Strong's Concordance* defines this as "to take pleasure in, to take delight in, to desire." This is so counter to the narrative many of us have heard. Part of why it seems so unreasonable is that we have a hard time with absolutes.

We are so used to minimizing, rationalizing, or excusing our failings that we can't grasp the idea of absolute holiness. But that is God—100 percent without flaw, totally perfect in every way. Our very best efforts will never be anywhere close enough to deserve God's acceptance.

The prophet said that "all our righteousnesses are like filthy rags" (Isa. 64:6). Paul had the same kind of image in mind when he wrote that all his religious zeal before he met Jesus meant nothing. All his supposed qualifications he now counted "as rubbish" (Phil. 3:8).

I know this is a bold statement, but it is a biblical one: the unregenerate man can do nothing but sin. Understand, sin is not confined to the common list of things we hear in church: lying, stealing, cheating, cursing, and all that. In fact, it often works itself out in nice, well-received, outwardly admirable ways.

Sin it not nearly as much an action of our hands as it is a posture of our hearts, and the greatest among us are still found lacking in the presence of a God who can see our hearts. If I'm honest, I have preached sermons and led altar calls while my heart was full of self-indulgent sin. I have stood on the platform of ministry, not in obedience or in submission to God, but because I loved the spotlight and the admiration it brought me.

Sin is simply an affront to God: He hates it so much that His only-begotten Son was covered in it and He was pleased to kill Him, to deal with it once and for all.

This is why Jesus sweat blood in the Garden of Gethsemane the night He was arrested. Certainly, the prospect of physical torment must have caused Him some anguish, but I do not believe this was the cup Jesus prayed to avoid.

Nor was the source of Jesus' great dread something you hear a lot in churches, that God the Father turned His back on Jesus when He was on the cross. The passage in Isaiah 53 doesn't say that it pleased the Lord to ignore Him. It says that it pleased the Lord to bruise or crush Him.

Taken alone, this is too much for us to be able to comprehend. Horrifying. But it comes into true perspective when we also see through the other lens of the View-Master: that God loves so much that He would go to these lengths to satisfy His righteous wrath and redeem us.

This is the intensity of our fierce, fearsome "I Am" God. He demands justice. He provides justice. He is our only hope—but He is the only hope we need. In Him we know both fear and delight.

Let's Pray

Father,
    In Your love for me, You have sacrificed more than I can ever imagine.
    Your fearful acts are driven by Your jealous love for me.
    I thank You for the privilege it is to be the prize for which You fight.
    I am Yours and You are mine, amen.

CHAPTER 12

THE WARRIOR KING

So shall they fear
The name of the Lᴏʀᴅ from the west,
And His glory from the rising of the sun;
When the enemy comes in like a flood,
The Spirit of the Lᴏʀᴅ will lift up a
standard against him.

—Isaiah 59:19

I like to tell stories when I preach, but I'm no Charles Dickens. While he gave us the classic *A Tale of Two Cities*, my offering here is a little more modest: it's a story of two houses.

One is the House of Peace. Dad built it, and our whole extended family lives there. It's a great place to be, full of joy and peace. Inside there is food and fun, safety and celebration. All our needs are met and all our dreams are exceeded in the House of Peace.

Next door is the House of Destruction. It looks good from the outside, and some of the rooms are nice enough, but there's one big problem: the place is marked for demolition. The wrecking ball is on its way, and that place is coming down, with anyone still in it to be buried in the rubble.

Knowing this, my Father has expanded the House of Peace. He's prepared plenty of room for anyone and everyone to come and join us. And accordingly, He's sent us out to go next door and extend an invitation.

That, in a nutshell, is the task Jesus entrusted the church with when He ascended into heaven. Somehow we have managed to make it more intimidating and complicated than it really is. That's not altogether surprising. When we lose sight of how utterly "other" God is—how scary—we don't just fail to worship Him as we should. We also fail to proclaim Him as we should.

When it comes to evangelism, much of the church has lost its way. We have allowed ourselves to be largely silenced by political correctness and by accusations of cultural insensitivity and religious intolerance. As a result, we're spending way too much time asking people what they want to hear from us, and way too little time asking God what He wants to say.

I believe the answer is in rediscovering the fear of the Lord. When we get a glimpse of how great and powerful and awesome Yahweh truly is, we won't be able to keep quiet because we don't know what to say or we don't want to risk offending anyone. When we see God as He really is, we will be emboldened to overcome any doubts, any insecurities, any worries that have kept us from stepping out to tell others about Him.

To do that, we have to know that our God is bigger than any and every enemy that might ever try to come against us. We must realize that it is not up to us to try harder, pray longer, sing louder, but that we have One who fights on our behalf: Jesus, the Warrior King.

When the Israelites reached the Red Sea after leaving Egypt, they despaired as they found themselves hemmed in by the water, with Pharaoh and his pursuing army coming up behind. There was no way they could get out of this, they thought.

Moses assured them: "Do not be afraid. Stand still, and see the salvation of the LORD, which He will accomplish for you today. For the Egyptians whom you see today, you shall see again no more forever. The LORD will fight for you, and you shall hold your peace" (Ex. 14:13–14).

OUR GOD IS BIGGER THAN ANY AND EVERY ENEMY THAT MIGHT EVER TRY TO COME AGAINST US.

I want to see more of that kind of faith in the church. The lust that has plagued you for so long? You'll never see it again! Those insecurities and fears that have haunted you because of abuse? You'll never see them again! Why? Because God will go to war on your behalf—and He will win.

Remember: God is the "LORD of hosts" in whose presence Isaiah cried out, "Woe is me!" (Isa. 6:5). Almost five hundred times in the Bible, the Hebrew word translated "LORD of hosts" is *tsaba*, which is defined as "army, war, warfare." It's not just what He does; it's who He is!

According to John, when Jesus returns, He will not be handing out high fives and hugs and making everyone feel better about their mistakes.

Now I saw heaven opened, and behold, a white horse. And He who sat on him was called Faithful and True, and in righteousness He judges and makes war. His eyes were like a flame of fire, and on His head were many crowns. He had a name written that no one knew except Himself. He was clothed with a robe dipped in blood, and His name is called The Word of God. And the armies in heaven, clothed in fine linen, white and clean, followed Him on white horses. Now out of His mouth goes a sharp sword, that with it He should strike the nations. And He Himself will rule them with a rod of iron. He Himself treads the winepress of the fierceness and wrath of Almighty God. And He has on His robe and on His thigh a name written: KING OF KINGS AND LORD OF LORDS. (Rev. 19:11–16)

Our God is a fighter! This is not just something He does from time to time. It is part of His nature and His identity, just as His description as Yahweh Rapha reveals Him to be a healer and Yahweh Jireh reveals Him to be a provider.

There is a great picture of our Warrior God in the familiar story of David and Goliath.

VICTORY IN THE VALLEY

Before we get to the warrior part, let's examine how the enemy works.

The Israelites and the Philistines were camped on either side of the valley, into which Goliath would stride each day and issue a challenge: "Choose a man for yourselves, and let him come down to me. If he is able to fight with me and kill me, then we will be your servants. But if I prevail against him and kill him, then you shall be our servants and serve us" (1 Sam. 17:8–9).

This left all the Israelites trembling, but wait a minute. Who decided this was a one-on-one, winner-takes-all contest? The Israelites were fooled into believing that one defeat had to mean they had lost the war.

Don't we do the same today?

"You had an affair, so God can never use you in ministry."
"You stumbled again. You're never going to get free of that bondage."
"You didn't do a very good job talking about Jesus. You should just keep quiet from now on."

These are lies. Just because you may have lost a battle, it doesn't mean you have to surrender the war. That idea is an old trick from a defeated enemy. Never accept those terms of engagement.

When we read about David and Goliath, we usually see ourselves in David's place, bravely going out to take on the giant because we know that God goes with us. There's a danger in doing this. We can end up making ourselves the hero of the story, rather than God. If we are not careful, we can become like Don Quixote, making more of our enemy that he really is so that we seem more heroic than we really are.

However, there's another way of seeing this account that gives God the starring role He deserves, and I believe provides a more theologically accurate interpretation of the story than the one we all heard in Sunday school.

Though he was a real person, David was also in many ways a prophetic representation of Jesus: he was a shepherd, a warrior, a king. It's why when Bartimaeus heard that Jesus was passing by outside Jericho, he cried out, "Jesus, Son of David, have mercy on me!" (Mark 10:47), and Jesus said, "I am the Root and the Offspring of David, the Bright and Morning Star" (Rev. 22:16).

And how did David come to be at the Israelites' camp to offer to go and take on Goliath? Like Jesus, he was sent by his father. Jesse packed David up and sent him to the front with supplies for his brothers, who were part of the army intimidated by Goliath's daily taunts.

We are much more like all those men than we are like David, if we are honest. It's one thing to go outside your tent with everyone else and shout at the enemy on the other side of the valley, as the Israelites did each morning. It's another to step down alone into the valley and face down the giant.

The real message of the story of David and Goliath is not that we are like David, stepping into the battle and taking down the enemy for God. It's that David is a prophetic type and shadow of Jesus, who came down to conquer the Enemy against whom we were all hopeless.

Look what happened after David cut off Goliath's head: "Now the men of Israel and Judah arose and shouted, and pursued the Philistines as far as the entrance of the valley and to the gates of Ekron. And the wounded of the Philistines fell along the road to Shaaraim, even as far as Gath and Ekron. Then the children of Israel returned from chasing the Philistines, and they plundered their tents" (1 Sam. 17:52–53).

When David won the victory, he gave everyone else the inspiration and the permission to pursue the enemy. Freed from fear and intimidation, the Israelites chased the Philistines all the way back to Gath—the hometown of Goliath, the one who had so terrified them. And they got to plunder the enemy's camp along the way. They were able to do all that not because of their own abilities, but because of what the young warrior king-in-waiting did on their behalf.

Jesus, our Warrior King, fights on our behalf, and He never loses. Our job is to rest in Him and the sufficiency of His strength. And as we learn to trust Him enough to live in rest, we will find ourselves positioned to arise with shouts of victory, to be bold and courageous, and to take back everything the enemy once had possession of.

A FEAR THAT COMPELS US TO GO

Please understand my heart. The call is not to run over and tell the neighbors in the House of Destruction that they are disgusting and shameful for living where and how they do. We don't need to criticize the way they have decorated. That's not love. While the gospel is offensive, we do not preach the gospel to offend, but to save.

But we must preach it! It is likewise not loving to simply ignore the danger in which the residents of the House of Destruction are living for the sake of avoiding offense. With a deeper understanding and experience of Hebrews 10:31—"It is a fearful thing to fall into the hands of the living God"—we will be more motivated to warn people of what's coming and tell them about the welcome waiting for them where we live.

When we go next door, we are not offering them fire insurance, however. We are not selling reinforced foundations. We are inviting our neighbors to come into the House of Peace because destruction is coming to them and they must come into safety now, before it's too late. We are asking them to leave everything they have built, everything they have known and loved.

Too often we talk about Christ as though He's an add-on to our lives, like He's an accessory that really sets off our favorite outfits or a sweet topping we pour on our favorite ice cream, something to make what's good just a little bit better. But He is so much more than that.

He is our only shelter from the coming firestorm. He is our only lifeboat in a raging sea. He is our only parachute in a falling plane. And equally important, He is the only door into purpose or peace. He doesn't simply save us from God's wrath; He saves us for God's glory! To keep that from anyone is not loving at all.

Remember how Jesus told His disciples not to be fearful of those who could kill them: "But I will show you whom you should fear: Fear Him who, after He has killed, has power to cast into hell; yes, I say to you, fear Him!" (Luke 12:5).

Paul wrote about how the knowledge that everyone is going to stand before Jesus one day in judgment propelled him: "Knowing, therefore, the terror of the Lord, we persuade men" (2 Cor. 5:11).

Many of us in the church are spending too much time worrying about what non-Christians might think about us if we talk to them about Jesus and not enough time wondering what might happen if we don't. Holding back from talking about Jesus to others isn't a sign of our respect for them; it's more like a sign of our indifference.

Don't just take my word for it. Here's what Penn Jillette, half of the hugely popular magic duo Penn and Teller—who is also an outspoken atheist—once had to say:

I don't respect people who don't proselytize . . . If you believe that
there's a heaven and hell, and people could be going to hell and
not getting eternal life, or whatever, and you think that, well, it's
not really worth telling them this because it would make it socially
awkward . . . how much do you have to hate somebody to believe
that everlasting life is possible and not tell them that?[1]

Part of the problem is that we have gotten fuzzy on the answer.
There's been a debate in some parts of the church in recent years about
whether hell really exists. And if it does, some have argued, then a loving God would never send any of His beloved children there. We're all
going to end up in heaven one day somehow, they say.

Let me put that to rest. There isn't the time or space to get into
a detailed discussion about all this here, but I hold to the orthodox
view that hell is a real place, where people will go if they have not
surrendered to the lordship of Jesus. Revelation 21:8 tells us that all
the "unbelieving, abominable, murderers, sexually immoral, sorcer-
ers, idolaters, and all liars shall have their part in the lake which burns
with fire and brimstone."

Furthermore, Jesus Himself said, "He who does not believe is
condemned" (John 3:18). Together, these verses make it pretty clear,
not only that there's a real place called hell, but also who will go there.

I believe it is also important to understand that hell is not the
Devil's dominion; it's his destination. Jesus made this clear when He
spoke about the coming of the Son of man: "Then shall he say also
unto them on the left hand, Depart from me, ye cursed, into everlasting fire, *prepared for the devil and his angels*" (Matt. 25:41 KJV). God
is as in control of what happens in hell as He is of what happens in
heaven. They are expressions of His love and His justice.

We won't all be in heaven because we're not all children of God,
as some like to say, though we are all created in the image of God.
But we can all *become* children of God. "But as many as received

Him, to them He gave the right to become children of God, to those who believe in His name" (John 1:12). In Galatians 3:7, Paul wrote, "Therefore know that only those who are of faith are sons of Abraham."

On Facebook, there are more than fifty ways you can identify yourself,[2] but Scripture talks about just two kinds of people: those who are adopted into God's family through faith in Christ and those who aren't. That's it; no middle ground. Paul referred to himself and the other believers as having been "enemies" of God before they were justified by Jesus' blood (Rom. 5:10). Now, if you're an enemy, you are, whether you are aware of it or not, in opposition to the work of God—and that's a very dangerous place to be.

That is what motivates me to tell other people about Jesus, to invite them to come into the House of Peace. There's an urgency to it, because we don't know when the day of destruction is coming.

Evangelism doesn't have to be a big production. I think of how my sons run next door and ask the little girl living there whether she wants to come outside and ride bikes. No drama. No fanfare.

The key to outreach is inclusion—we are not asking people to fix themselves; we are asking them to join our family. It may be messy. It may be difficult. They may bring some of the culture of their old house into the House of Peace, but we are going to work it out together and fight for each other. That's what family does.

THE GOSPEL IS THE ONLY HOPE

I'm reminded of the imminence of the House of Peace's end every time I think of a young guy I met after one of our shows in Waco, Texas. He hung back behind a couple of friends he'd come to the concert with as Candice and I spoke with them.

This couple talked about some of their hurts and heartaches, and we told them how much God loved them and would never fail them. They let us pray for them, that God would make Himself known to them in a real way. It was a sweet moment.

Afterward, the two of them turned to their friend and asked if he'd like to pray as well. I told him how much God loved him and that he didn't have to have all the answers worked out—he could just ask God to show Himself to him if He was real.

For a moment something like "maybe" flickered across his face. Then the shutters came down again.

"No, man," he said. "I'm my own God."

That was okay, I told him, no pressure. "I'm not mad at you, man," I said. "Just want you to know that we really do love you."

Then, after hugs and encouragements for the couple we had spoken with to look out for how things were going to change for them now that they'd connected with God, the three of them headed home.

Only they didn't make it. A couple of days later, I got a phone call from Gabe, who had booked the show. He said that he'd been told the three of them had been in a car accident on their way back from the show.

The couple were in the hospital, Gabe said. They were banged up, but they were going to be okay. Their friend, who'd flipped the vehicle when he took a curve too fast, had died at the scene.

Just minutes after rejecting an invitation to consider Jesus, this young man was dead. I don't know what happened in his mind or heart in between leaving us and failing to make that turn, but I do know the last thing he had spoken to me was a rejection of God.

For him, there likely wasn't time to reconsider; that's a heavy thing to think about.

I'm not just driven to tell people about Jesus by an awareness of the seriousness of what's at stake, though. It's not only that I want them to avoid destruction, but it's also that I do not want them to miss out on the absolute blast it is living in the House of Peace.

A believer with whom I'm acquainted challenged me about the way I always preached the gospel so fiercely at For Today shows. "You know, Mattie, most of these people here are not Christians," he said at a gig. "You're making them feel uncomfortable."

I answered, "But the gospel is the only hope they have. Even if they hate the gospel, it is still their only hope."

He came back at me. "Mattie, you talk about hearing the voice of God . . . What if God doesn't want you to do it every day like this? What if one day God doesn't want the crowd to hear the gospel?"

I thought for a minute before responding. "Well then," I said, "He shouldn't have sent me."

I look at it this way: Why would Yahweh send me there if He didn't want people to hear about His wonderful love for them? Why would God send you into that coffee shop if there weren't people there He wanted to hear too? Psalm 37:23 says, "The steps of a good man are ordered by the LORD."

If you are born again and filled with the Holy Spirit, God wants to speak to you and to direct your steps. Wherever I go, I try to remember that I am there on purpose—on an assignment from God—and I seek to be open to His leading.

I'm reminded of the prayer by Jim Elliot, one of the five missionaries martyred in Ecuador in the 1950s: "Father, make of me a crisis man. Bring those I contact to decision. Let me not be a milepost on a single road; make me a fork in the road, that men must turn one way or another on facing Christ in me."[3]

I know a common hesitation is that most believers feel unqualified to share the gospel—like, they're not proficient enough with Bible verses or persuasive enough in their presentation. But sharing can be as easy as just telling someone that Jesus loves him or her. I've had people dismiss that as a waste of time, but I have seen God use that simple phrase in powerful ways many times.

I remember being in a mall in Australia with a group of guys with whom I had been speaking at a conference. They were sharing the gospel with someone while I sat nearby, watching them. Close by was a little old lady, probably in her seventies, weighing no more than a hundred pounds. What caught my eye was the bottle of whiskey under her arm.

I turned to her and said, "Hey, do you know Jesus loves you?"

She gave a sort of half laugh and answered, "Oh, I sure hope so!"

I felt God whispering to me that she hadn't really heard what I said. So I leaned in a little farther and looked her in her eyes. "No," I said, "I mean He really loves you."

This time her face changed. I saw a flicker of pain.

"I just don't know," she said. "I have lost so much in my life. My best friend just died two weeks ago, and all I have left is this." She held up the whiskey.

A bunch of Bible verses and testimonies came to mind, but none seemed right. I found myself being overwhelmed with a fatherly love for this woman, who was old enough to be my grandmother. I stood up, reached out, and pulled her into a hug. She kind of disappeared in my arms.

We stood there quietly for a few seconds, a bit of an awkward tableau in the mall. Then I began to feel her shake, and the sobs started to bubble up and overflow. Grabbing the back of my shirt in her small hands, she bawled into my chest for several minutes.

Now I was wondering what to do: preach, pray, prophesy? *Don't do anything*, God said. *You're just the door I'm walking through.*

So I just stood there holding this woman whose name I didn't even know until her tears subsided. Eventually she pulled back, wiping her eyes and her nose. I sat down to be level with her and took her hands in mine. Looking into her face, I said, "Sweetheart, do you want to give your life to Jesus today?"

"More than anything," she said. And we prayed right there, in the mall.

Then there was the crazy time someone was offended when I did *not* tell her about Jesus . . .

I was getting off the plane when I passed two flight attendants at the door, a guy and a gal, saying goodbye to all the passengers. I turned to the man as I passed and said, "Hey, Jesus loves you so much."

He thanked me, and I added, "Bless you, man. God see you through the day," as I left.

I caught up to the friend I was traveling with, who had stopped in the hallway to pray for someone he'd gotten into a conversation with on the flight. As I waited for him to finish, the two flight attendants I'd just passed came up behind us.

The male steward dropped something behind him, so I called out to let him know. He turned and went back to retrieve it, leaving his female colleague standing near me.

I turned to her. "Jesus loves you a lot," I said.

She looked a little taken aback and turned to her colleague. "He said it!" she excitedly told him with a big smile on her face.

He came up to us. "Did you tell her Jesus loves her?" he asked.

"Yeah."

"Man, she was so upset when you didn't say that to her before," the man went on.

My ignoring her had apparently caused her to wonder, *What about me? Why didn't he say that to me? Does God love me too?*

We stood and talked there in the hallway. I told her that maybe it was all no accident, what had happened. "God is after you," I said. "He made sure I got the chance to tell you."

Her eyes filled with tears. "I've been looking for something more," she said.

Then I shared the gospel with her, and she was born again.

In both cases, the door at the House of Destruction was opened through simply saying, "Jesus loves you" (even belatedly!). Anyone can do that.

That conviction was part of what led me to leave For Today after ten years. I loved what I was doing, and it was thrilling to see God use us to reach a group of young people who, for the most part, had rejected the traditional church. They saw it as judgmental and irrelevant. We were able to show them not only that Jesus loved them but also that He had the power to break the chains that held them and heal the wounds that incapacitated them.

At the same time, I saw that we could not do it all on our own. Evangelism isn't supposed to be left to a select few. The Great Commission is the whole gospel to the whole world by the whole church.

That's what led to me to launch Awakening Evangelism. My dream is that we can help inspire and equip countless Christians around the world to share the good news fearlessly in any situation, to make God the center of attention, and to have an eternal impact on the world around them, through radical love, relentless courage, and timeless truth.

I believe we'll be ready and willing and able to do this when we know more of God as the great Warrior King.

Let's Pray

My God,

You are my champion, my great Warrior King.

You fight for me the battles I never could have hoped to win on my own.

Use me to share the good news of Your victory boldly, and to show a scared world what a fearless church really looks like, amen.

CHAPTER 13

THE STRONG MAN

But the Lord your God you shall fear; and He will
deliver you from the hand of all your enemies.
—2 Kings 17:39

In some of the places For Today played, there was a real clash of kingdoms. You could sense the collision of light and darkness. I used to spend a lot of time fighting the Devil in dark, sweaty venues.

I'd throw myself into the show as if it were a heavyweight bout. I even wrote a song about it all, "Devastator." It was one of our most popular songs, including these lines:

> *Hell, fear me. I am the one that will bring you down.*
> *And when you fall, feel me.*
> *You'll see my face on the battleground.*

Since being led into a life centered more in the fear of the Lord, I have changed a bit. I still believe there's conflict between light and dark. I just have a different view of my part in it all.

I have realized that I don't have to fight for God. He doesn't need my help in defeating the Devil. Colossians 2:15 declares, "Having disarmed principalities and powers, He made a public spectacle of them." Think about that. The demonic forces against which so many of us have wrestled and warred were disarmed and publicly humiliated by Christ.

When Jesus was on the cross and had received the sour wine held up to Him, "He said, 'It is finished!' And bowing His head, He gave up His spirit" (John 19:30). At Calvary, Jesus defeated death, the Devil and his works once and for all.

Sometimes, however, it seems to me that we have misinterpreted that verse to read, "It is started . . . and things will be wrapped up one day, if you can give Me a bit of help."

But no, Jesus said it was *finished*. Done. Complete. The work of freeing us from sin and reuniting us with God was over. The cross was sufficient. We don't need Jesus and something else—whether that's this new spiritual discipline, or five years of counseling there, or that prescription medicine.

Please do not misunderstand me. This is very important. I am not saying there is no place for counseling or spiritual disciplines; nor am I saying there is no place for prescription medicine. I have availed myself of all of these in the past.

What I am saying is that while God may choose to use them in your life, He does not need to. The cross was sufficient. As a result, I don't have to fight for God, to help Him finish the job. Rather, God fights for me. And the way I position myself to be won by Him is to lay down my sword and simply seek His face.

There's a wonderful illustration of what I mean in the 2014 movie *The Hobbit: The Battle of the Five Armies*, directed by Peter Jackson.

Bard the Bowman is trying to protect the people of Lake-town from Smaug the dragon's attack, but the monster is too fierce. Bard and everyone else seems doomed, until his son, Bain, appears with the only thing that can stop Smaug: a large, black steel arrow.

Fashioning a crude bow between two posts at the top of a tower, Bard rests the arrow on his son's left shoulder as he takes aim. With his back to Smaug, hearing the snarling threats and feeling the heat of the advancing dragon, Bain starts to turn his head to see what's happening.

"Bain," Bard says softly but sternly, "look at me. You look at me." The boy turns back and locks his eyes on his father's.

As he focuses on the weak spot in Smaug's underbelly that he needs to hit, Bard tells his son, "A little to the left."

Bain moves slightly as directed, and Bard lets the arrow fly, straight into Smaug's heart. Father and son embrace as the dragon falls to its death.

That's how I engage in spiritual warfare now. It's not that there isn't conflict; it's just that the conflict is never my focus.

DON'T GIVE THE DEVIL TOO MUCH CREDIT

I have spoken in churches where before the service the leaders huddled to pray and would spend several minutes rebuking and yelling at the Devil and never even talk directly to God. Then they just ended with, "In Jesus' name, amen," and that was it. They may have felt fired up, but I wonder how effective they were.

In fact, I think the Devil is very happy about this kind of approach. Why? Well, first, because he gets the attention—the desire for which led to his fall. But more important, because, as my spiritual father has said for years, "the Devil will let you chase him around a tree stump all day long, if it will keep you from engaging the Father."

The Devil doesn't want God to get the glory and attention that are His because he knows what will happen if He does. So, he tries to keep us distracted and diverted from a pure pursuit of Yahweh—the one thing that matters.

There is also a subtle danger in believing that God needs our help. We can end up becoming the hero of our lives, rather than God. Satan's greatest goal is not always to get us to worship him. Sometimes it's to get us to follow his lead by worshiping ourselves. He wants us to believe in ourselves more than we believe in God. Self-adoration—that's how his fall came about.

Some of the spiritual warfare talk I hear in the church gives way too much credit to the Devil. He's nowhere near as powerful as they make him out to be. He is just very good at bluffing—like that little old guy behind the curtain in *The Wizard of Oz*. Evangelist Reinhard Bonnke calls the Devil "a mouse with a microphone"[1]—he roars pretty loud, but he's nothing to be afraid of when you see him for who he really is.

Isaiah wrote about how Lucifer was cast down from heaven for seeking to "be like the Most High" (Isa. 14:14). He also foretold of his coming end, and how his bluster would be exposed: "Those who see you will gaze at you, and consider you, saying: 'Is this the man who made the earth tremble, who shook kingdoms, who made the world as a wilderness and destroyed its cities, who did not open the house of his prisoners?'" (vv. 16–17).

Actually, the Devil has more reason to fear us than we do him.t "He who is in you is greater than he who is in the world" (1 John 4:4). Who is in us? Jesus, the Warrior King, before whom demons fall and beg for mercy, burying their faces in the ground, as Moses and Isaiah did.

In fact, Paul implored us to remember that our bodies are "a temple" of the same presence that killed Uzzah, and Aaron's two sons—the physical presence of the same God that answered Elijah by fire and gripped John with fear (1 Cor. 6:19).

For me these days, spiritual warfare has more to do with my ears than with my lips. It's not so much about what I pray, or say to the Devil, or how much of the Bible I can quote. It's about listening to God and doing what He tells me. Sure, that may be to pray or to quote the Bible, but it will be effective not just because I did it but because it's what God directed me to do.

This may seem like a subtle distinction, but it's a huge shift in emphasis. I want Yahweh to act more than I want the Devil not to act. More of God isn't only better than less of the Devil; it also inevitably means less of the Devil. Switch a light on and the darkness has to give way.

The powers that be were threatened when the early church exploded in numbers after Jesus' resurrection, so much so that they hauled Peter and John before them and ordered them not to speak about Jesus anymore. We don't know exactly the threats they made (Acts 4:17), but given that Peter and John had not long before seen Jesus crucified, they must have known that their lives were on the line.

It is instructive to see how they responded. They did not bind the enemy or beseech God to still him. They gathered their friends and turned their attention to God, declaring, "Lord, You are God" (v. 24).

Then they prayed, "Now, Lord, look on their threats, and grant to Your servants that with all boldness they may speak Your word, by stretching out Your hand to heal, and that signs and wonders may be done through the name of Your holy Servant Jesus" (vv. 24, 29–30).

God's answer to the prayers of Peter and John and the others in Acts 4 wasn't to provide a formula for overcoming fear; it wasn't a six-week online course on how to become spiritually confident. It was this: "The place where they were assembled together was shaken; and they were all filled with the Holy Spirit, and they spoke the word of God with boldness" (v. 31). *That* was God's answer for a scared, weak church—more of His presence, more of His Spirit, more of His power. More of Himself.

We find all this in the House of Peace. When we come into God's place, we come under His protection. Where Jesus is, there is peace, not disorder. There is confidence, not doubt. There is hope, not despair. In His presence there is no uncertainty, no indifference, no confusion.

JESUS: THE ULTIMATE STRONG MAN

Many Christians are familiar with the concept of the "strong man" Jesus spoke about in Mark 3. Usually, though, it's only seen as a reference to some demonic presence or principality, and how we need to bind the work of hell in people's lives if they are to be set free.

However, the principle is broader than that. Jesus wasn't speaking specifically or exclusively about the Devil or hell. For those of us living in the House of Peace, our watchman is Jesus! The Devil did everything he could to overcome Him and failed. Not only was the Devil unable to keep Jesus tied down by death, but He also returned with the keys to hell and the grave.

That means we can confidently quote Romans 8:31: "If God is for us, who can be against us?" Because standing at our door is the unconquered, unchallenged, matchless, incomparable, undefeated Champion of the multiverse. Who could ever challenge us if we are hidden in Him?

And so now, when I'm engaging in "spiritual warfare," I focus on the Father, and I try to respond to what He tells me ("A little to the left!"), knowing that He, like David facing Goliath, is the One who fights on my behalf: "Do not be afraid. Stand still, and see the salvation of the LORD . . . The LORD will fight for you, and you shall hold your peace" (Ex. 14:13–14). His call is for us to do great things *with* Him, not great things for Him.

I feel I should offer a word of caution here. While I believe we need to focus on what God tells us to do, I am not suggesting that "God said" should take precedence over Scripture. The Bible remains our foundational authority. God's spoken Word, as perceived in our spirits, will never contradict or detract from His written Word. He doesn't change, and neither will the personality and priorities He displays so clearly in Scripture.

In fact, we should be very cautious about claiming God's direction. This is, after all, a book about the fear of the Lord. And it's no small thing to put words into God's mouth! It's a holy, precious moment when the all-powerful Creator of the universe speaks to us individually, and we should never trivialize that. Far better to say, "Hey, I have an idea; let's try this," than to casually state, "God told me to . . ." if you are not really sure.

However, if some Christians may be a bit overconfident when it comes to saying that God told them to do something, I have found that far more have the opposite issue. They say that God never speaks to them. I have lost count of the number of times I have heard through the years, "I just can't hear the voice of God."

I don't think that's really the case, though. I think what's happening is that He *is* speaking, but these folks are just not recognizing it. Unfortunately, we have developed some false expectations about what it means for God to "speak" to us. We think it has it be some big, earth-shattering encounter. But more often than not, it's probably going to be something smaller and quieter, like, *You missed that chance to speak with kindness and grace to your spouse today. You need to ask for forgiveness and set it right.*

Thing is, if we're honest, we like to hear the dramatic direction God may have for us, but we're often less open to hear His quiet correction. After taking on the prophets of Baal on Mount Carmel, Elijah feared for his life and fled to the mountains. Huddled in a cave, he cried out to God. The answer came:

And behold, the LORD passed by, and a great and strong wind tore into the mountains and broke the rocks in pieces before the LORD, but the LORD was not in the wind; and after the wind an earthquake, but the LORD was not in the earthquake; and after the earthquake a fire, but the LORD was not in the fire; and after the fire a still small voice. (1 Kings 19:11–12)

We need to be willing to hear God whatever He has to say, knowing that it is for our good and His glory. We can be quick to cry out to Him to deliver us from depression or divorce or from poverty or persecution. But are we as desperate for Him to deliver us from self-preservation, from self-centeredness, from self-promotion, from self-justification? Far too often, we ask God to deliver us from some enemies, while we keep others around as pets!

I still believe we need to fight for truth and for justice. My part in this war, however, has taken on a different meaning for me. In his famous passage on spiritual warfare, Paul urged, "My brethren, be strong in the Lord and in the power of *His might*" (Eph. 6:10). The secret to victory isn't my intensity, how fierce I am; it's intimacy—how *near* I am to the Father.

The only authority the Enemy has in our lives is that which we give him. James 4:7 says, "Submit yourselves, then, to God. Resist the devil, and he will flee from you" (NIV). We beat the Devil by turning from him and giving our attention to God. And when I am close enough to Him, I can hear Him tell me how—or *if*—He wants to use me in the battle.

THE SECRET TO VICTORY ISN'T MY INTENSITY, HOW FIERCE I AM; IT'S INTIMACY.

I'm struck by how often in the Bible God does things in ways that don't make much sense to us. When Joshua led the Israelites to besiege Jericho, a well-fortified city, they laid down their arms and walked around the walls in silence once a day for six days. Then on the seventh day they made seven circuits and finally burst into shouting and song. What a crazy-sounding idea—but the walls fell down.

When Gideon took on the Midianites, he whittled his volunteer army down to a handful and swapped weapons for a pot and a torch and a trumpet. Again, what a crazy-sounding idea.

As perhaps God's most successful warrior king, David might have been forgiven for thinking that he knew how to do things. But he didn't lose sight of the fact that he needed to follow God's directions above his own experience. Having taken back Jerusalem from the Jebusites and united Israel, David became a threat to the Philistines. When they came out against David, he asked God, "Shall I go up against the Philistines? Will You deliver them into my hand?" (2 Sam. 5:19).

God said yes, and David went and routed the Philistines, but they were not done. They regrouped and came back. David could easily have figured he knew what to do this time: what had worked the last time, of course! But he knew enough to check first with God, who had other ideas:

> He said, "You shall not go up; circle around behind them, and come upon them in front of the mulberry trees. And it shall be, when you hear the sound of marching in the tops of the mulberry trees, then you shall advance quickly. For then the LORD will go out before you to strike the camp of the Philistines." And David did so, as the LORD commanded him; and he drove back the Philistines from Geba as far as Gezer. (vv. 23–25)

WITHOUT WISDOM, ZEAL CAN GET OFF TRACK

One of the biggest dangers to those who love God and want to serve Him is confusing our zeal with God's will. We must never forget that "unless the LORD builds the house, they labor in vain who build it; unless the LORD guards the city, the watchman stays awake in vain" (Ps. 127:1).

Otherwise we end up doing things God never intended and not getting around to the things He did have on His heart for us. Perhaps the best example in the Bible of a man rightly prioritizing God's voice above human ambition is in Acts 8, when Philip went to the city of Samaria and a revival broke out. There were miracles of healing and deliverance as God moved in power, and "there was great joy in that city" (v. 8). As something of a hub of that part of the world, the city was poised to be a significant gateway for the gospel.

Who wouldn't want to be part of that, right? Faced by that sort of opportunity, many of us would probably do everything we could to make the most of it: bring in more workers, arrange more meetings, hold training events to pass on what we have learned so others can do the same thing somewhere else. Or maybe take out a loan for $10 million so we can build a building big enough to fit all the people.

I've seen many great ministers become slaves to momentum. They find themselves always compelled to "strike while the iron is hot," and they end up determining the direction of their ministry based on the enthusiasm and opinions of their congregation, instead of the leading of the Spirit of God.

Not Philip. An angel of the Lord came to him and told him, "Arise and go toward the south along the road which goes down from Jerusalem to Gaza" (v. 26). I love how the verse then adds simply by way of explanation, "This is desert." Lots of dust, but no people.

Many of us would question whether we had really heard right. After all, God wants revival—salvation, miracles, freedom from bondage, right? That's all happening in Samaria. Why on earth would anyone walk away from that to go out into the middle of nowhere? It just makes no sense.

We have the advantage of history. We know how it all turned

out—how Philip met the eunuch from Ethiopia, who was riding past in a chariot, and how he led the man to faith in Christ and baptized him at the side of the road. It's widely believed that this eunuch was responsible for taking the good news back to Ethiopia, where the church flourished. With the gift of hindsight, it all makes sense.

But Philip was not told any of this. He wasn't given any details about how things would turn out. He was just told to do something that did not make much sense—and he obeyed. In doing so, the kingdom of God was advanced in ways that could not have happened had he stuck with what he knew and what seemed to be more obviously God's work—including casting out demons.

We need to have the same kind of attitude today. We need to be more attuned to what we hear than what we think we know. We need to be willing to say yes, even when it's something as counterintuitive as shutting down a citywide revival to go for a walk through the desert.

When God first spoke to me clearly back in 2006, it wasn't with a big plan, even though He may have had one in mind for me. He didn't tell me I was going to move to Iowa to join this metal band and that I would tour the world and preach the gospel in stadiums.

He said, *Mattie, you need to deal with your porn addiction. You need to delete from your phone the numbers of those people you used to party with. You need to start waking up earlier and giving some serious time to reading My Word. You need to go to church more.*

I started to work on all that, and in due time He led me to the "big" stuff. And then, after a decade of touring the world and performing for hundreds of thousands in a job that many would kill to have, He said, *Walk away.* With no plan for the future and no promise of "big" stuff ever again, I obeyed. I learned from Philip that the place of obedience is much better than the place of influence.

Only the heart content with surrender can truly rest in the victory of Jesus. I have met many leaders in ministry who are exhausted by the system of religious activity; they are beaten down by the constant drive to perform, to produce, and to promote. Yet their hearts ache for the truth of a God who steps down into the battlefield on their behalf—one who invites them to enjoy the fruits of the House of Peace while He stands watch at the door.

THE PLACE OF OBEDIENCE IS MUCH BETTER THAN THE PLACE OF INFLUENCE.

If we will allow ourselves to engage God like this, we will find that He, like Bard the Bowman, is able to use us to conquer the dragon, not by our own effort or might, but by simply remembering His Word: "Look at Me."

Let's Pray

Lord,

You are victorious in all things, and I trust You with my life.

No one can challenge You.

Help me to see You standing at the door to my heart, that I might live forever in the House of Peace, amen.

CHAPTER 14

HOW TO LIVE IN FEAR

Therefore you shall keep the commandments of the
Lord your God, to walk in His ways and to fear Him.
—Deuteronomy 8:6

At the end of the service, people were lying all over the floor of the church. Some were weeping. Some were laughing. Some rolled around in glee while others were still and soulful. God was there.

But to be honest, I wasn't feeling it. I'd enjoyed hearing the visiting speaker tell of the amazing things that had happened when revival hit his church some years before. He spoke of miracles and marvels and how God's presence was so strong that people came from all over the world, lining up around the block for hours to get a seat for a service.

When the visiting pastor prayed, some of that same sense of God fell on the meeting I was in, but my mind was elsewhere. I'd come because I was supposed to meet some old friends who were going to be there, to talk about a book they were working on. Now I needed to get to the hospitality room at the back of the church, where we'd arranged to connect. Only trouble was, getting there was like navigating an obstacle course.

Though I had not really been personally touched by what had happened in the service, I knew that others had. I could see that God was at work, and I was pleased for that. And I didn't want to get in the way, to interrupt what He had in mind for each person.

So, I gingerly made my way through the crowd, careful not to step on anyone. I was wearing my keys clipped onto my belt loop, and I pressed my hand against them so they did not rattle. I held my breath so as not to disturb the peaceful atmosphere.

Then it occurred to me: I was walking differently because I knew God was near. I was acutely aware of how everything that I did might impede His intentions, and I did not want that to happen.

I was reminded of something Damon Thompson, whose ministry I have appreciated for years, talks about—how, when Jesus was baptized by John in the Jordan, the Holy Spirit descended on Him "like a dove" (John 1:32). The Bible doesn't say that the Holy Spirit took the form of a dove, Damon notes. Rather, the Holy Spirit was dovelike, with characteristics similar to the gentle bird.

That means that if I want the presence of God in my life, I must live as though there's a dove sitting on my shoulder. I'll be very careful about what I do, so as not to frighten it away.

R. T. Kendall, the respected Bible author and teacher, made the same point. He even warned of the danger of confusing a pigeon with a dove. They may look the same from a distance, but they are very different. He wrote:

> You can train a pigeon; you cannot train a dove. The pigeon can
> be domesticated; the dove is a wild bird. A pigeon is belligerent;

the dove is loving. A pigeon is boisterous; a dove is gentle. A pigeon will mate with more than one pigeon; the dove mates with only one dove for life.

The pigeon represents the counterfeit spirit—strange fire. The dove represents the Holy Spirit—holy fire. I reckon there are services where people imagine that the Holy Ghost came on the church, but when you get to the bottom of it, you discern it may be pigeon religion. Strange fire.[1]

As I've said, since that night God scared me in the trailer, I have had some similar experiences, but I don't live there. It's not an everyday occurrence. I do not always have that heart-racing, overwhelming sense of the here-and-now, fearsome holiness of Yahweh. But I choose to live in the light of that reality, even when I do not physically experience it.

Here are seven keys I have found for anyone wanting to become more aware of God's presence. These will provide some structure or direction if you are longing to create an environment that welcomes and embraces the fear of the Lord and positions you for the wonderful blessings that come with it.

1. ACKNOWLEDGMENT: RECOGNIZING GOD'S SOVEREIGNTY

First, we need to be clear about who's in charge. There is a God in heaven, and we are not Him! He is absolutely 100 percent holy. He is utterly pure. He is totally and always right; He is unfailingly just. He never does anything wrong. He is completely without fault.

It may not always look or feel that way to us, the way the world is today, but guess what! That just means we don't see the big picture yet. I am not saying this to minimize anyone's pain or struggles, and

God does invite us to pour out our honest hearts to Him, our disappointments and frustrations. He wants us to be real with Him.

But we do so from a position of knowing that God declares, "For as the heavens are higher than the earth, so are My ways higher than your ways, and My thoughts than your thoughts" (Isa. 55:9).

We need to decide that we don't have to understand. We just have to obey—to stay positioned, eyes locked with His in intimate wonder, no matter how dire the situation around us. That's the only way we can ensure that we hear it when He whispers, *A little to the left.* We trust Him when it doesn't make any sense, and we obey Him when we don't see the why or the what. When God speaks, we respond.

When I found myself with three days between ministry commitments in Tulsa, Oklahoma, rather than head home to be with my family, as I usually would, I felt prompted to check into a hotel on my own for some time just with God. I was excited about what lay ahead, wondering whether there might be another life-changing encounter like that one in the trailer, or some life-defining direction or revelation He might give me in that dedicated time of prayer.

Reaching the door of my room, I sensed God telling me, *Take off your shoes and leave them by the door.* I did so, feeling a bit like Moses in front of the burning bush. *Hang up your jacket in the closet. Fold your clothes when you take them off, and make your bed when you get up in the morning.*

I made a mental note and got settled with great anticipation and a bit of nervousness. And then—nothing more. For the next three days, I kept my room as straight as if I were a new recruit in military boot camp, waiting for a surprise inspection of the barracks. I folded my clothes perfectly, made my bed so well it looked like it had never been slept in, and wiped down the counters every time water touched them. But there was nothing more, no great experience of God. I learned a great lesson, however. If I expect to play host to God's presence, it will require me to meet His presence with my best—in both behavior and belief.

When we truly acknowledge who God is, we will also be careful not to take His name in vain. It is a commandment, after all. This doesn't mean just being careful not to use it carelessly in speech. It means being careful not to misrepresent it to others.

As Christians we take on the name of God as a woman typically takes her husband's last name when she marries; the two are identified together. In the same way, everything we do and say should acknowledge our belief in and relation to a holy, perfect God. That should cause us to be very careful about how we represent ourselves—and Him.

2. AVAILABILITY: SAYING YES TO GOD'S PRIORITIES

This may not sound very spiritual, but some things just take time. Some churches, services are run so tightly that it seems to me God can't get a word in edgewise. We create systems and structures and then invite God to "move freely"—as long as He does so within the boundaries we give Him.

But He doesn't always work on our timetable. In fact, I've found that often the fear of God is most evident when we've given Him room to move outside of our schedules, structures, and systems.

When the service has run two hours and forty-five minutes and 80 percent of the congregation has left, that's not uncommonly when God shows up and begins marking people in the most significant way. He comes for those who have waited, those who have tarried in His presence, telling Him, "God, I'm after this, and I don't want to leave until I know that I know that You've touched me." That's often when He shows up with the most decisive, destructive, devastating power.

Why does God work this way? It's not because He's messing with us. It's because what He has to offer is too precious to give carelessly. It's because He wants us to decide that we are really hungry, that we are truly thirsty. He wants us to let go of everything else.

After all, when it comes down to it, we give time to what matters most to us. How much time do you give to God each day? I don't mean in doing things for Him, but just being with Him, sitting in His presence, reading His Word, or worshiping Him. There's an old saying that goes, "Children spell love T-I-M-E." Well, in some ways, so does Yahweh.

Availability doesn't mean just telling God that He can call you anytime and then getting on with what you want to do. That's passive faith. Being available to God means actively waiting on Him, pursuing Him, ready to do whatever He may ask, but willing to just sit and gaze upon Him in His majesty.

You may say you're too busy, but I'm not so sure. Yes, we all have responsibilities: work, school, family, just the daily stuff of living. But chances are, if you keep a detailed record of what you do with your time for a week, you'll find a lot of it goes to nonessentials. Facebook, anyone?

One way to make yourself available is to switch off. Your phone. Your computer. Your television. Cut out the distractions. Give God your undivided attention.

I have a prayer room in my home. It's a bedroom I've converted into a meeting place with God. There's a chair and a desk, a bookshelf with some Bibles and devotional reading, a speaker to play worship music, and a big beanbag to lie on. That's it.

I used to have this room as my office too. But I found that I'd go in to pray, see some bills on the desk that needed paying or some paperwork that needed attending to, and I'd get busy with that instead of being still before God. So the office got moved elsewhere.

Now when I step through the door into my prayer room, I'm making a statement: "I'm here, God, for You." When I close the door, I'm leaving everything else behind me.

Remember what Jesus told His disciples: "But you, when you pray, go into your room, and when you have shut your door, pray to your Father who is in the secret place; and your Father who sees in secret will reward you openly" (Matt. 6:6).

3. ANTICIPATION: EAGERLY AWAITING GOD'S OPPORTUNITIES

You may have heard the statement, "God loves you and has a wonderful plan for your life." But have you ever stopped to think what that might look like if it were actually true, like in an actual day-to-day way?

It's not just that God has a plan for you sometime in the future, but maybe even today, even this morning. His plan is not just for your career or who you might marry somewhere down the line, but the people you meet as you go about your regular life right now.

When I close the door to my prayer room, I do so with a sense that *from here on anything could happen*. If I am really making myself available to God, then there are no limits. And I come out of that prayer room on a mission. With a purpose.

Being available to God means that wherever you go and whatever you are doing, He can interrupt. He can direct or redirect you as He best sees fit. How might you walk differently if every time you went into a building, a room, a situation, you realized, *God put me here*?

One time I was at a music venue called the Red Door in Pensacola, Florida, for a show. For Today wasn't on the bill; we'd gone to see some other bands that were friends of ours. Still, I went with the same kind of sense of anticipation that I'd have when we went onstage.

During the evening, I had this feeling that I should go and stand on the other side of the room. So, I made my way over there slowly, checking for a sense of when I was in the right place, as if I were following an inner GPS app.

Finally, I got to what I felt was the right spot. Almost immediately, someone came up to me and slapped me on the arm.

"Hey, are you Mattie Montgomery?"

I smiled and told him yeah, I was.

If I'd stayed where I was, chances are we would not have met. But this guy said his name was Luke, and we got to chatting. We stepped outside to talk some more. I got to hear his life story and his struggle with drug addiction, and a little while later I got to lead him into the saving knowledge of Christ as His Savior. All because I'd gone to stand on the other side of the room.

Some Christians get really hung up about finding out what their unique "calling" in life is. Does God want them to become a missionary or campaign for an end to slavery or run a successful business?

Yes, all those things matter to God, but those are not *all* that matters to God. I'm also not so sure it matters to Him who goes and does it. At least, that's what I see in the case of Isaiah.

In many Bibles, the passage in chapter 6 where Isaiah sees the glory of God's throne room is titled "The Call of Isaiah," or something like that. But that's not accurate. Isaiah wasn't called to be a prophet here; actually, he'd already been prophesying for five chapters.

Furthermore, God didn't call him to go here; Isaiah volunteered when God asked, "Whom shall I send, and who will go for Us?" Isaiah enthusiastically responded, "Here am I! Send me" (v. 8).

Isaiah's going on behalf of God wasn't necessarily *his* calling; it was *anyone's* calling. Anyone who was willing to say yes to it.

> BEING AVAILABLE TO GOD MEANS THAT WHEREVER YOU GO AND WHATEVER YOU ARE DOING, HE CAN INTERRUPT.

There's an old saying that "God isn't looking for ability; He's looking for availability," and it's still true. Now, I do believe that God has a plan and purpose for every life, but if you don't step up and engage it,

He isn't going to wait around forever. Leonard Ravenhill said, "The opportunity of a lifetime needs to be seized during the lifetime of the opportunity."[2] God will take that opportunity from you and give it to someone else. Your calling is given, but it is not *a* given.

Does that sound too severe? Remember the parable of the talents in Matthew 25. Each of the three servants had an individual assignment given to them by the master, fitted to their abilities. Yet in the end, the master took the talent he had given to the third servant, which the servant had failed to use, and gave it to one of the others.

As I've written before, For Today wasn't the greatest band around. I don't believe we were God's first choice to be the most influential Spirit-filled metal group of the last decade or so. There were a number of other, more talented outfits out there, who played better and put on better shows and were better positioned to carry that torch.

But as they grew in popularity, they started to wobble. Then came the drugs, the indiscretions, the doubts and subtle rebellions that grew into disbelief. The secular music scene is a tough place; over time it swallowed them up. Some of those other bands broke up and some of them just gave up, in the sense of losing their zeal for being a witness for Christ; they just drifted into run-of-the-mill music careers. None of them made the impact for God they could have—or should have.

That left For Today, a group of guys who were committed to pursuing integrity and giving God all they had and could. I'm not saying that our efforts made us successful; they just put us in a place where God would use us successfully.

We must keep in mind the lesson of the third servant in the parable of the talents and remember that when God gives us something, He expects it to be used well. His gift may look like a calling. An opportunity. A talent or an ability or a resource. And there is a weightiness to His calling that can only be carried appropriately when we are walking in the fear of the Lord.

We can get sidetracked by worrying too much about our calling. Instead of fretting about the future, let's be open to God using us here and now. I heard of a pastor who told members of his congregation that they may not know what their calling is right now, but that didn't have to stop them from being on call each day—available to whatever opportunity presented itself. I like that.

God may call you to go overseas one day, but He may just want you to take the long way home from work today, open to the unexpected. Like turning off your phone, being open to God asking or doing the unexpected means letting go of control and letting God be in charge.

4. ATTENTIVENESS: LISTENING TO GOD'S DIRECTION

I once heard a great definition of multitasking: doing a bunch of things poorly at the same time. You see, the fact is, we're not like computers, which can have lots of programs open and still just hum along.

Some states have introduced laws that prohibit people from texting while driving because of the number of accidents caused by people messing with their phones while behind the wheel. But researchers have found that even just talking on the phone while driving can affect your responsiveness.[3]

Think about when you're on the phone in a coffee shop. You may be able to hear some of what the person on the other end of the line is saying, and some of the chatter of those sitting around you, but you're not really going to catch all of both conversations. You have to choose who you are going to listen to. It's the same with God. We need to make an effort to tune in to Him.

Part of the answer is to shut off distractions, making ourselves available in some of the ways I have mentioned previously.

Now, some people tell me they'd love for God to use them to

touch people they come into contact with in their everyday lives, but they just don't hear God speak to them clearly. My answer to them is, first, don't get hung up about the idea of hearing God's voice. Some people have told of hearing an actual, audible voice, but that's not usually it.

My friend Elijah, who works with me at Awakening Evangelism, puts it really well: "Most of the time, when I say I heard God's voice, it's not that I actually heard God's voice, it's that I thought God's thoughts."

So be more attentive to your thoughts, and if you suspect they have been placed there by God, then act on them. Maybe it is something that is prodding you to step out of your comfort zone. If so, that could well be God, because when you do something that is beyond you, you have to rely on Him, and He is going to get the glory, right?

I can already hear you asking, "But how do I know if that thought is from God?" Consider this: Charles Spurgeon wrote, "We declare, on scriptural authority that the human will is so desperately set on mischief, so depraved, so inclined to everything that is evil, and so disinclined to everything that is good, that without the powerful, supernatural, irresistible influence of the Holy Spirit, no human will will ever be constrained towards Christ."[4]

If that is true, then we must also acknowledge that a random thought that pops into our heads to pray for a stranger, or to share the love of God with the waitress at a restaurant, never could have come from our human will!

Scripture clearly teaches that the human heart, left to its own devices, would never choose to glorify God at the expense of its own beloved comfort. Before Jesus brought us to new life, "we all once conducted ourselves in the lusts of our flesh, fulfilling the desires of the flesh and of the mind, and were by nature children of wrath, just as the others" (Eph. 2:3).

So you can rest assured and obey confidently, knowing that the thought you had that would bring glory to God must have been placed there by the Holy Spirit. Unless He put it there, you simply don't have that in you.

But if God says A, don't wait for B and C. They may not come until you step out, like when I wandered across the floor at the Red Door. Maybe it will turn out great, or perhaps it might end up in a bit of a mess. Maybe nothing notable will happen at all, but either way you are going to learn something about yourself, and about God. And what a rush when He does use you to do something unexpected or unplanned.

Over time you'll find yourself getting more comfortable in stepping out, more confident that it's God who is speaking. Remember what Jesus said: "My sheep hear My voice, and I know them, and they follow Me" (John 10:27).

Keep in mind, too, that sometimes God might speak to you through someone else. Your friend or coworker or the person next to you in the line at the grocery store may say something that is an invitation to you to speak to them about God.

I try to go through my day with my ear sort of half-cocked, listening for what God might be saying wherever I go.

5. SUBMISSION: ACCEPTING GOD'S GOVERNANCE

This area is probably the hardest for people to accept, especially for my generation. We live in a culture that increasingly rejects the idea of leadership and submission. We don't want anyone telling us what we can and can't or should or shouldn't do . . . from the president to the police to our parents or pastor.

We are constantly on the lookout for examples of poor or abusive leadership so we can point the finger and say, "See, that's why I don't submit. That's just not right."

I'm not talking about blind allegiance. We shouldn't stay where there is actual harm or willful heresy. But too often people head for the door—of relationships or churches—just because their feelings get hurt.

That's not God's design. He has established order and authority on the earth. We talk about being part of the army of God but seem to forget that in an army you are going to get told what to do. Imagine what would happen in the military if every time an officer gave a command, his troops got into a huddle to discuss how everyone felt about that and hold a vote.

"Honor your father and your mother" is one of the Ten Commandments (Ex. 20:12), remember, not a suggestion. We are instructed to pray for our leaders—not gripe about them on social media (1 Tim. 2:1–2).

If there are things that we don't like or don't agree with, what might happen if we spent less time talking to others about it all and instead talked to God? Even better, spent time listening to what He might have to say?

We like the idea of Jesus being our Good Shepherd, but shepherds who are good at their job don't just make sure the sheep get fed, free them when they get tangled in thickets, and go looking for them when they get lost. They also nudge them into line with a big stick. Maybe the word *nudge* is a little too gentle.

David—the shepherd boy who became a king—talked about how God's rod and staff comforted him (Psalm 23). But a shepherd's rod is specifically designed to bring discomfort. David had used his to strike sheep if they began to wander off, so how could that be comforting to him? Because he knew that the rod and staff of his heavenly Shepherd would keep him safe, turning him from the path of destruction back to safety.

I know that I need that in my life, someone looking out for me. It was what brought me to the church home I have found here in Mobile.

As For Today started to gain popularity, the crowds at our shows grew. Where there had been a handful, there were scores, then hundreds. Our sphere of influence expanded—and along with it came greater responsibility I knew I was not strong or wise enough to handle on my own.

Then a friend I respected said he had been praying for me about all the doors that were opening up and felt he should connect me with Apostle Aaron Smith. I reached out to him, and Apostle Aaron came to one of our concerts. When we talked after, I sensed a genuine interest in and concern for me from him.

He wasn't after anything, unlike some other pastors I'd heard from, whom I sensed thought it might be cool for them to be associated with an edgy, popular band like For Today. Apostle Aaron just wanted to offer what he could to what he saw God was doing through my life. I knew I wanted, needed, to be part of a church with that kind of pastor.

I've gladly submitted to his leadership because I recognize his wisdom and I trust his heart. I've given him permission to talk straight to me. When he speaks, I listen. I don't always understand his thinking and sometimes I don't even agree, in the moment, but I submit to his leadership because I trust him and because I believe God has placed him in a position of authority over me.

A young man came to spend some time with me because he saw me as some kind of a mentor, and I invited him to church with us. I introduced him to Apostle Aaron, who called me the next day or so.

"I don't want you to spend any more time with that young man," he said simply.

I didn't ask why. I didn't disagree. I didn't say I'd think about it or pray about it. I just submitted and obeyed and trusted God to use Apostle Aaron for my good. He went on to explain that he'd sensed something dark about the guy, something spiritually violent. A rebellious and hateful spirit that was out to get me and my family.

Sure enough, some months later we heard that the guy had gone off the rails, emotionally, verbally, and physically abusing his girlfriend and falling away from God, rejecting and attacking the other Christian leaders in his life. Because I was submitted to the rod of authority God had placed in my life in the form of Apostle Aaron, my family and I were spared being caught up in it all.

6. SURRENDER: SUBMITTING TO GOD'S CORRECTION

A dear friend of mine called the other day, in trouble. He was engaged to be married to a great young lady, but he'd just confessed to her that he'd been sending sexually explicit messages to someone else. He realized that everything he really wanted was now on the line.

"Get over here," I told him.

When he arrived, he explained everything that had happened. Give him his due; he didn't try to sugarcoat things.

I listened. I asked a few questions. Then I let him have it.

"We don't do that here," I told him sternly. "This is not what you and I represent."

I didn't downplay things and try to make him feel better. I told him how dumb he'd been, and he agreed. Then I told him that he was better than that, and he agreed. Then I told him he could and would do whatever it took to rise above this, and he agreed.

He knew that I wasn't calling him out. I was calling him up, up to be the man he truly desired to be, up to the life he really aspired to. I could speak straight to this dear friend because we love and trust each other. We had been through the fire in ministry. We'd watched each other's backs before, and he knew I'd do anything to see him succeed—even if it meant hurting him.

We all need people like that in our lives, people we can be open and honest with. Real friends. A great Bible teacher once defined a friend as "someone who loves you but isn't impressed with you."

Those kinds of relationships don't just happen. They have to be pursued. You have to be intentional about committing to and connecting with the right people. Christians like to quote Proverbs 27:17—"As iron sharpens iron, so a man sharpens the countenance of his friend"—but don't always like to acknowledge that requires close proximity. It can't be done at a distance.

I am glad to be in relationship with a group of people who I know love me enough to be real with me, and who I trust to be open and vulnerable with. They'll talk straight to me if I am off base or out of line. They'll call me on my stuff, lovingly but firmly. They'll encourage me when I need it and correct me when I need it.

Chief among them is Candice, who knows me best, of course. She's close enough to see my faults and failures more clearly than anyone else. But she has also heard more of my dreams and desires, my hopes and my passions. She knows who I really am and who I really want to be, and she is committed to seeing those two men meet.

When I find myself getting distracted or discouraged, she is there to remind me. "I know the man you are supposed to be, and you're moving in the wrong direction right now," she'll say. She may be only four foot eleven and just around a hundred pounds, but you can be sure that when she speaks, I listen!

7. SURROUNDINGS: ALIGNING OUR ENVIRONMENT WITH GOD'S STANDARDS

We are affected by our environment more than we often realize. Candlelight and soft music may be pretty clear indicators that "love is in the air," as the old song goes, but things are not always so obvious.

There's a science to the way retailers lay out their stores, the way they light them, and the music they play. They know they can create mood and desire in shoppers without them even noticing.

The lesson from all this: we need to be really careful about our surroundings. Remember the old story about the frog in the kettle. Supposedly it jumped into the water and didn't realize that someone had switched the kettle on. The temperature rose gradually, boiling the poor unsuspecting frog to death.

We need to watch where we go. I'm not going to suggest a list of specific places you need to avoid, because it's not so much about what is going on outside, around you, as what's going on inside.

With For Today, I spent a lot of time in some grungy places, but I wasn't there as a tourist. I was there on a mission. If God sends you into a dark place, then go with boldness—remember that "He who is in you is greater than he who is in the world" (1 John 4:4). But you need to be honest with yourself about whether you're going into the darkness with purpose and vision from God, or if you're just curious about what goes on there.

We also need to watch what we let into our hearts and minds: "Keep your heart with all diligence, for out of it spring the issues of life" (Prov. 4:23). The idea is that we should have a barrier, where everything that wants to come in has to stop to be checked. Many Christians don't have this in place, I have noticed. Instead, they have a big banner that says, "Come on in, all welcome!"

What kind of music do you listen to? What sort of movies and shows do you watch? Do you pause to ask God if you should play that song or tune in to that program? Are you open to switching them off if you sense His nudging to do that?

I love movies, really love them. I often find God speaking to me through them, showing me some symbol or parable that speaks so much about life and His kingdom—like the way Bain and his father defeated Smaug the dragon. I sometimes refer to them when I speak.

But there are times when I reach for the remote because I sense God telling me, "This is not for Us, Mattie."

When people want to get fit and get in shape, they are very careful about their diet. They read the labels to check the ingredients and choose items that they know will be good for them. If we want to become spiritually fit, we should do the same with our entertainment diet.

That doesn't have to mean only listening to "Christian" things. While I do not only watch "Christian" movies, I will only watch ones that God will watch with me. I want His presence and guidance as I watch anything. And if there is something on the screen that is offensive or insulting to God, the last thing I would ever do is to say, "Listen, God, You're not going to like this part. How about You leave me alone and we'll catch back up later?"

We should feed ourselves only that which is going to enrich us, not leave us feeling bloated and nauseous. Ask yourself whether your media diet passes the Philippians 4:8 test:

> Finally, brethren, whatever things are true, whatever things are noble, whatever things are just, whatever things are pure, whatever things are lovely, whatever things are of good report, if there is any virtue and if there is anything praiseworthy—meditate on these things.

Will all these things mean you will experience the fear of the Lord in your life in the same way I did in that prayer room in Virginia, all those years ago? Not necessarily. There is no single set formula, no one best recipe, no unique right prescription. This is not about following a set of rules. It is about intentionally seeking to create an environment that welcomes the fear of the Lord and embraces and positions you for the wonderful blessings that come with it.

We don't know a lot about what the early disciples did after Jesus told them to "wait for the Promise of the Father," before He ascended to heaven (Acts 1:4). But we do know that when the Day of Pentecost came, "they were all with one accord in one place" (2:1).

That certainly sounds like somewhere where there was availability, anticipation, attentiveness, submission, surrender, and an alignment of their surroundings to God's standards and ways. And the result— the Holy Spirit came with tongues of fire and forever changed the course of human history.

Let's Pray

Father,

I incline my heart and surrender my life to the awareness of Your holy presence.

I remove distractions and turn from deception, that I might see and hear You more clearly.

Overwhelm me with Your glory, and use me to reveal Your heart to the world You died to save, amen.

CHAPTER 15

JESUS WINS

The fear of the LORD is clean, enduring forever.
—PSALM 19:9

I f you have been around church for any length of time, you have probably heard a preacher make the statement, "I've read the end of the book, and I know who wins." It may be overly familiar and have lost some of its impact on us, but it's still true. Jesus wins. He is and always will be King of kings.

In ancient times, a robe was a symbol of a king's authority and rule. It's said that victorious kings would cut off part of the robe of the enemy kings they vanquished and add it to their own, as a sign of their power and authority. So when the prophet Isaiah wrote that the train of the Lord's robe "filled the temple" (Isa. 6:1), he was making a statement about God's supremacy and all-sufficiency.

In describing the complete work of Jesus' death and resurrection,

Philippians 2:9–11 says, "Therefore God also has highly exalted Him and given Him the name which is above every name, that at the name of Jesus every knee should bow, of those in heaven, and of those on earth, and of those under the earth, and that every tongue should confess that Jesus Christ is Lord, to the glory of God the Father."

This doesn't mean that everyone ought to acknowledge Jesus as Lord, in a wishful-thinking, wouldn't-that-be-nice kind of way. It means that one day everyone will. It is going to happen.

God stated it clearly: "I have sworn by Myself; the word has gone out of My mouth in righteousness, and shall not return, that to Me every knee shall bow" (Isa. 45:23).

No one is going to stand before God and argue with Him that He has been unfair to them, so they deserve a pass, or that they have been good enough to warrant His mercy. In the full intensity of His presence, everyone will acknowledge His perfect fairness and justice.

Trouble is, many Christians seem to doubt this. They look around at all the terrible things going on in the world, and they see the difficult things going on in their own lives, and they can't reconcile what they read in the Bible with what they see and experience.

I get it. When I was a boy, my dad loomed large in my life. Not just physically, but in every way. He was my hero. There were so many things he taught me about life and God—like through that encounter with Brock.

I was just eight when my father died of cancer. It was really hard watching him suffer. Toward the end, he'd lost the weight and strength that so amazed me when I was younger. He wasn't the great protector and the bad-guy defeater I'd come to know. He was a sick, broken, dying man without even the strength to roll himself over in bed.

Some tough years followed. I'd grown up in church and always heard that God was good and how much He loved me, but it was difficult to reconcile that with losing my father in such an ugly way.

He had been a good man, a faithful church member, a hard

worker, a loving husband, a caring father. Why did he have to suffer like that? Why did I have to lose him? For a time I was really angry about the injustice of it all, and I let the world know it. I got some counseling and was even given medication for a time. They helped, but they weren't the answer. That didn't come for some time.

My loss caused me to question what I thought I knew, setting me on a road to find out more. And the answer I finally came to: Jesus wins.

I don't mean this glibly, or to ignore other people's hurt. But through coming to understand and experience something more of the immensity of who Yahweh really is, through embracing the fear of the Lord, I can say confidently today that, in the end, Jesus wins.

He is the undisputed, all-sufficient Champion of the galaxies, reigning over everyone and everything. And because I have been crucified with Christ and so no longer live, but Christ lives in me (Gal. 2:20), all the fullness of who He is and what He has done is available to me. He is in me and I am in Him. My hurt is His hurt, and His victory is my victory.

NO SURRENDER, NO DEFEAT

Even in His death, Jesus won. He sat in absolute authority, even as He hung on the cross. His life was not taken from Him there at Calvary; He gave it up willingly. "And when Jesus had cried out with a loud voice, He said, 'Father, into Your hands I commit My spirit.' Having said this, He breathed His last" (Luke 23:46).

It's easy to miss if you read this passage quickly, but this is not usually how people died when they were crucified. Death by hanging on a cross was terrible and tortuous. It was slow suffocation. As the strain on their bodies increased through the hours or sometimes days, those being executed would struggle for every breath, as my dad did.

Not Jesus. While anyone else would have been fighting for their next breath, getting weaker and feebler, He was able to cry out with a loud voice. When He said, "Father, into Your hands I commit My spirit," He wasn't surrendering. He wasn't giving in. He was *commanding His spirit to leave His body.*

Even on the cross He was in total control. His passing was so different from what normally happened at these executions that the centurion on duty "glorified God, saying, 'Certainly this was a righteous Man!'" (v. 47).

I don't believe that the Devil is behind every bad thing that happens in the world. He's not that capable. Sometimes bad things just happen; that's part of living in a fallen creation. However, the Devil is a great opportunist. He does try to take advantage of bad things by making us wonder and question and doubt.

I still don't know why my dad died. Well, I know it was cancer, but I don't know why our prayers weren't answered in the way that we hoped. But because of what He did, I believe that even in death, Jesus wins. He makes all things serve Him.

When Jesus heard that His dear friend Lazarus was sick, He delayed a couple of days before returning to Lazarus's home in Bethany. On learning about His friend's condition, He said, "This sickness is not unto death, but for the glory of God, that the Son of God may be glorified through it" (John 11:4).

This seems odd, because Lazarus was so sick that he did die. Jesus would later bring him back to life by calling him out of the tomb. Just as He would command His own spirit to leave His body not long afterward, here He commanded Lazarus's spirit to return to his body.

The word *unto* here in the phrase "not unto death" means something a little different from the way we usually use it. It conveys the sense of being "for the advantage of." And that changes our understanding of what Jesus said.

Did this sickness that Jesus had been told about lead to Lazarus's death? Yes, it did. But did this same sickness give death an advantage? No, it most definitely did not.

Jesus had raised the dead before this, but this was even more dramatic. Lazarus had been dead for four days by the time Jesus arrived in Bethany; his sister Martha even warned that his corpse was probably already starting to stink.

When Jesus called for the stone blocking Lazarus's grave to be removed and summoned Lazarus from inside, He wasn't only reaffirming His power; He was signaling His own resurrection to follow a few days later.

Death may have thought it had won when it—temporarily—claimed Lazarus, but it had not. Jesus won. And that remains true to this day. It is why Paul wrote, "And we know that all things work together for good to those who love God, to those who are the called according to His purpose" (Rom. 8:28).

Some people wave this verse around lightly, I know, but it's true nonetheless. God took the sting of death in Lazarus's life and used it to demonstrate to every bystander that God the Father had sent Him (John 11:42). God took the sting of death in my life and turned an eight-year-old's loss into a source of strength, through which I have had the opportunity to tell others about Yahweh's great and fierce love.

GOD USES EVEN THE WORST FOR OUR BEST

Because of what I have been through, I believe I can say with confidence and authority that the worst that life can possibly throw at us can be used by God to draw us into deeper intimacy with Him, so that we can experience and share more of His glory.

Sometimes God uses difficult things to awaken us to who He really is, as He did with Job. You'll often hear Job referred to as a wonderful example of faith, but I am not so sure that's the real message to be found in his story.

The Bible describes Job as "one who fears God and shuns evil" (Job 1:8). This may be notable, even commendable, but nowhere do we read that Job actually knew or loved God. He was not described as a "friend of God," like Abraham was, or a "man after God's own heart," like David was. He was simply a man who was afraid of God, and because he was afraid of God, he didn't do bad things. But fearful obedience without intimacy is superstition. And sadly, there's a lot of Christian superstition in the postmodern church.

When Job's idea of how the world works—"I do the right thing, God blesses me, and I have a happy life"—was turned upside down, he was forced to press in. He turned to God and asked, "Who are You really, because I don't think I know!"—the same question I had after my father's death.

God answered Job's questions with questions of His own that gave him reason to be fearful. "Who is this who darkens counsel by words without knowledge?" He began (Job 38:2), following that with four chapters of questions that make it plain just how mighty and vast God is, and how small and insignificant Job was in comparison.

Awed by what he had been shown of God's infinite majesty, Job's only response was a fear that led to repentance: "I have heard of You by the hearing of the ear, but now my eye sees You. Therefore I abhor myself, and repent in dust and ashes" (42:5–6).

What I see in this story is not just a wonderful picture of a relationship based on godly fear replacing one based in human effort, but of God's good heart to people.

We know that "the LORD blessed the latter days of Job." He gave him a new family and He doubled his livestock holdings (vv. 12–13). Without having come to know God personally, though, I believe this additional prosperity would have been a curse rather than a blessing—it would only have heightened Job's superstitious sense of having to do the right thing. It would have deepened his commitment to spiritual superstition, and he would have been even more content to live outside of the place of intimate encounter.

In His great love, God used Job's suffering to position him for more. The lesson I come away with from reading Job's story is that even the Enemy's best efforts to destroy you can serve you if you will commit yourself to seek God in the midst of trouble.

I was like Job in the sense that, after my dad died, I had to come to the place of saying, "I thought that I knew You, but I guess I really didn't."

I still don't know why my family's prayers for Dad weren't answered. I still don't understand why some people are healed and some aren't. But I do know that God is able to heal and God is willing to heal, whether I see it with my eyes or not. Jesus always wins, even if it sometimes takes us a while to be able to see or say that.

I refuse to let my inability to have all the answers stop me from believing that He is the answer to everything and that His Word is true—that the prayers of the faithful can heal the sick, and that we are to go and cast out demons, raise the dead, and free the prisoners—all in the name and power and authority of Yeshua Jesus, our great Warrior King and the unmatched Strong Man standing at our door.

Psalm 24:1 says that "the earth is the LORD's, and all its fullness"—*is*, not *will be* or *could be* or *might be* someday after the Rapture happens. Is. Even though it may not always seem that way.

In one of His parables, Jesus said that the kingdom of heaven is like a treasure hidden in field "which a man found and hid; and for joy over it he goes and sells all that he has and buys that field" (Matt. 13:44). This is gold buried in the dirt. It makes me think of God's promise in Isaiah 45:3: "I will give you the treasures of darkness and hidden riches of secret places." Is the gold any less valuable because it's a bit grimy? Not for a moment. But it required someone to give everything that he had to bring it out.

That was what Jesus did in establishing His kingdom on earth. He paid the price for every soul who has ever lived and who ever will, each one unique and precious and marvelously valuable, however much they may seem to be covered in dirt.

Jesus' death and resurrection weren't just about securing us a place in heaven. They happened so we might be part of bringing the reality of the heavenly dimension to earth right now. "For the grace of God that brings salvation has appeared to all men, teaching us that, denying ungodliness and worldly lusts, we should live soberly, righteously, and godly in the present age" (Titus 2:11–12). In other words, we don't have to wait for the age to come to live as God intended. We can start now, because He has the answer to all that would prevent us from living as He intended.

You name it, and there is an answer in Christ.

Sickness? He healed the lepers, made the blind see and the lame walk.

Death? He raised Lazarus, and the widow of Nain's son, and through His resurrection broke the power of the grave.

Demonic oppression? He delivered the Gadarene demoniac, the boy who had fits that caused him to fall into the fire, and many more.

Shame? He broke its grip off the woman at the well and the woman caught in adultery.

Anything that the Enemy or the fallen world tries to throw at you, Jesus carried it to the cross and buried in the ground, once and for all.

When Jesus took all my sin with Him to the cross, there went my fallen inclinations, my weaknesses, my tendencies to sin. There went my desires and my ideas about life, about what it means to be a man and what it means to be successful. Everything went at the cross, not only my guilt.

My life can now be an outworking of Galatians 2:20: "I have been crucified with Christ; it is no longer I who live, but Christ lives in me; and the life which I now live in the flesh I live by faith in the Son of God, who loved me and gave Himself for me."

And Jesus does not lose. Because of this, because of the complete victory Jesus has won, we can smile bigger, dance harder, and sing louder. The fullness of the Christian life is a celebration of the finished work of the cross.

The cross is our redemption, but it is also the ultimate expression of God's intense hatred for all that mars the beauty of His perfect creation. It's His fierce love and loving fierceness meeting in harmony.

Only with a deeper awareness and experience of God's utter holiness and otherness, one that strikes fear—*yare'*—into our hearts, can we ever really appreciate the depth and richness and freedom of His incomparably great love for us.

Finding God to be scary doesn't need to drive you away from Him; it should draw you closer in the knowledge that, in Christ, all of God's matchless intensity is not set against you but is set against all that is against you.

Knowing that the fear of the Lord frees us from any and all other fears should give us confidence to step out into the world in hope and faith and love, expectant of good things and filled with purpose.

We are equipped for this not because of our eloquence or our intelligence, or by our good works or good looks, or through our Bible memorization and methodologies, or as a result of our charisma. Our only qualification is that our great Warrior King is with us, before us, and within us—and thankfully that is the only qualification we could ever need.

The mistakes of your past have not disqualified you from the glory of your future, if, trembling, you will leave them on the altar to be consumed by the firestorm of God's holiness. This is the fear of the Lord that brings freedom. Everything we do now can flow from the great wonder and deep joy this discovery brings. Your victory was won two thousand years ago on a cross just outside Jerusalem. It really is finished. Jesus really does win. And anyone who says otherwise will have to deal with your big, scary Dad.

Watch out, Brock!

Let's Pray

Yahweh, my Father,

I see You now for who You truly are.

You are the one true God—beyond compare, seated above every other authority and power, and matchless in praises.

Keep me awestruck in Your wonderful presence, that I may never give my attention or affection to another.

You are worthy to be exalted, and I will honor You as my King forever—starting right now, amen.

AFTERWORD

I mentioned in this book how I love to hear stories about how people encounter God in a new way, discovering more of His fire and fury and His love, and about their being propelled into the world to share that wonderful reality with others.

If God has shown more of Himself to you through reading *Scary God*, I would love to hear from you! You can share your story by writing to me at info@mattiemontgomery.com. For speaking and other inquiries, you can contact me at booking@MattieMontgomery.com.

As you walk in this new revelation of the fear of the Lord, you can find resources to further equip and encourage you at our Awakening Evangelism website, www.awakeningevangelism.com. There you'll find a blog, testimonies, articles, videos, opportunities for service, and more.

Additionally, you can find us on

FACEBOOK: WWW.FACEBOOK.COM/AWAKENINGEVANGELISM
INSTAGRAM: @AWAKENINGEVANGELISM

You can follow me personally at

WWW.FACEBOOK.COM/MATTIEMONTGOMERY
INSTAGRAM AT @MATTIEMONTGOMERY

ACKNOWLEDGMENTS

I have been privileged to walk through this *Scary God* season of my life with a small group of wonderful people who are unwaveringly devoted to truth, and fiercely committed to me. Chief among them is my wife, Candice—my partner in crime—whom I'd like to thank for her strength and support. To be her husband is the greatest honor I have in life, and I believe today more than I ever have before: we can do anything. Also, my three sons, Kai, Caleb, and Carver, for reminding me that no matter what needs to be done, playing outside is still very important work.

I'd like to thank my spiritual father, Apostle Aaron Smith, and his wife, Pastor Robbie, for their steadying influence and direction in my life. Thanks also to Dr. Mark Eckel, John Bevere, Michael Koulianos, Corey Russell, and Joy Dawson for being powerful voices from whom I drew much inspiration and insight while preparing to write this book.

Thank you to Cody Van Ryn and Joel Kneedler from Emanate Books for being willing to take a chance on me, and finally, thanks to the illustrious Andy Butcher for walking with me through this process with such brilliant patience and perspective.

You are all real-life superheroes, and my life is brighter for having you in it.

NOTES

INTRODUCTION

1. Charles Spurgeon, "Self-Humbling," *Spurgeon's Sermons*, vol. 13 (1867), Christian Classics Ethereal Library, https://www.ccel.org/ccel /spurgeon/sermons13.xxi.html.

CHAPTER 2: THE TWO SIDES OF FEAR

1. Sara G. Miller, "1 in 6 Americans Takes a Psychiatric Drug," *Scientific American*, December 13, 2016, https://www.scientificamerican.com /article/1-in-6-americans-takes-a-psychiatric-drug.

2. Jack Craver, "Study: Americans Spending 10 Percent of Income on Health Insurance," BenefitsPro, October 27, 2016, http://www .benefitspro.com/2016/10/27/study-americans-spending-10-percent -of-income-on-h.

3. Rob Cain, "2017 Is the Biggest Year for Horror in Decades," *Forbes*, October 16, 2017, https://www.forbes.com/sites/robcain /2017/10/16/2017-is-the-biggest-year-for-horror-in-decades /#7042ffd752d9.

4. Mark Eckel, "Horror (Part Two)," *Warp and Woof* (blog), May 20, 2014, https://warpandwoof.org/horror-part-two/.

5. Mark Eckel, "MONSTERS: Why Are We Attracted to Fear?" *Warp and Woof*, October 29, 2012, https://warpandwoof.org/monsters/.

6. A. W. Tozer (@TozerAW), "A Scared World Needs a Fearless Church," Twitter, July 12, 2014, 11:44 a.m., https://twitter.com/tozeraw /status/488031079672983552?lang=en.

CHAPTER 3: THE FRUITS OF GODLY FEAR

1. John Bevere, *The Fear of the Lord* (Lake Mary, FL: Charisma House, 2006), 177.
2. Joy Dawson, *Intimate Friendship with God: Through Understanding the Fear of the Lord*, rev. ed. (Grand Rapids: Chosen Books, 2008), 23.

CHAPTER 4: FEAR IS A FOUR-LETTER WORD

1. Awr Hawkins, "CDC Report: 35,369 Vehicle Accident Deaths, 505 Gun Accident Deaths," Breitbart, May 1, 2015, http://www.breitbart.com/big-government/2015/05/01/cdc-report-35369-vehicle-accident-deaths-505-gun-accident-deaths.
2. Dawson, *Intimate Friendship with God*, 21 (see chap. 3, n. 2).
3. John J. Parsons, "The Awe of the Lord," Hebrew4Christians, accessed April 25, 2018, http://www.hebrew4christians.com/Scripture/Parashah/Summaries/Eikev/Yirah/yirah.html.

CHAPTER 5: MOSES: A MAN WHO FEARED GOD

1. "Bull Cults in Ancient Egypt," accessed June 4, 2018, https://www.ancientegyptonline.co.uk/bullcult.html.
2. Dawson, *Intimate Friendship with God*, 31 (chap. 3, n. 2).

CHAPTER 7: THE BIBLE IS FULL OF FEAR

1. Bevere, *The Fear of the Lord*, 158 (see chap. 3, n. 1).

CHAPTER 8: THEN AND NOW: THE FEAR OF THE LORD ENDURES

1. Jonathan Edwards, Sinners in the Hands of an Angry God: a Sermon, Preached at Enfield, July 8, 1741, at a Time of Great Awakenings; and Attended with Remarkable Impressions on Many of the Hearers (New York: printed by G. Forman, opposite the post-office, for C. Davis, no. 94, Water-Street, 1797).
2. *The Life of the Reverend Mr. Jonathan Edwards*, http://www.digitalpuritan.net/Digital%20Puritan%20Resources/Edwards%2C%20Jonathan/%5BJE%5D%20The%20Life%20of%20the%20Reverend%20Mr.%20Jonathan%20Edwards.pdf.

3. Jonathan Edwards, with S. E. Dwight, *The Works of President Edwards: With a Memoir of His Life* (n.p.: 1829), 1:592.

4. Edwards and Dwight, 162.

5. Edwards and Dwight, 161.

6. Edwards and Dwight, 162–63.

7. Edwards and Dwight, 167.

8. Duncan Campbell, *Revival in the Hebrides* (1949), 4–5, http://www.tracts.ukgo.com/campbell_revival_hebrides_sermons.pdf.

9. Campbell, 5.

10. Campbell, 5.

11. Campbell, 5–6.

12. Campbell, 6.

13. Campbell, 7.

14. Campbell, 10.

15. Campbell, 23.

16. Bevere, *The Fear of the Lord*, 8 (see chap. 3, n. 1).

17. Bevere, 9–10.

18. Bevere, 11.

19. Bevere, 11–12.

20. Bevere, 13.

21. "Special Guest—Joy Dawson—March 6, 2016," YouTube video, 1:33:08, posted by Water of Life Community Church," March 9, 2016, https://www.youtube.com/watch?v=02M04JDrVu4.

22. "Special Guest—Joy Dawson."

23. "Special Guest—Joy Dawson."

CHAPTER 10: GOD'S KINDNESS AND SEVERITY

1. Bevere, *The Fear of the Lord*, 95 (see chap. 3, n. 1).

2. Bevere, 177.

3. Bevere, 22.

CHAPTER 11: FEAR AND DELIGHT

1. A. W. Tozer, *The Knowledge of the Holy* (New York: HarperCollins, 1961), 1.

CHAPTER 12: THE WARRIOR KING

1. Penn Jillette, "I Don't Respect People Who Don't Proselytize," BeliefNet, posted by Susan Johnson, accessed April 27, 2018, http://www.beliefnet.com/columnists/reformedchicksblabbing /2009/11/penn-jillette-i-dont-respect-p.html.

2. Leslie Walker, "How to Edit Gender Identity Status on Facebook," Lifewire, updated December 19, 2017, https://www.lifewire.com /edit-gender-identity-status-on-facebook-2654421.

3. Jim Elliot, personal journal, quoted in Elisabeth Elliot, *Shadow of the Almighty: The Life and Testament of Jim Elliot*, reissue ed. (New York: HarperCollins, 2009), 59.

CHAPTER 13: THE STRONG MAN

1. Reinhard Bonnke, official Facebook page, May 25, 2015, https://www.facebook.com/evangelistreinhardbonnke/photos/a.10150 417025670258.624699.210552700257/10155488539210258/?type=3& theater.

CHAPTER 14: HOW TO LIVE IN FEAR

1. R. T. Kendall,"Why Nothing is Worth Grieving the Holy Spirit," Identity Network, accessed April 27, 2018, http://www.identitynetwork.net/apps/articles/?articleid=89944.

2. Quoted in Rick Joyner, "We Need More Men of God Like Leonard Ravenhill," *Charisma*, October 22, 2015, https://www.charismamag .com/spirit/revival/24688-we-need-more-men-of-god-like-leonard -ravenhill.

3. "Driving and Talking on the Phone Is Much More Distracting Than Previously Thought, Even with a Hands-Free Device," https://www .bustle.com/p/driving-talking-on-the-phone-is-much-more-distracting -than-previously-thought-even-with-a-hands-free-device-8418976.

4. Charles Spurgeon, "Human Inability: A Sermon (No. 182)," March 7, 1858, the Spurgeon Archive, http://archive.spurgeon.org /sermons/0182.php.

ABOUT THE AUTHOR

Mattie Montgomery is the founder and president of Awakening Evangelism, a ministry that provides instruction and support to believers from all around the world who desire to grow in their ability to share the gospel and advance the kingdom more fearlessly in their everyday lives.

After first stepping onto the stage of international ministry during his ten-year stint as the vocalist of renowned Spirit-filled hardcore band For Today, Mattie developed a passion to serve the body of Christ as an author, speaker, and instructor. It is his joy to train, equip, and inspire believers to join with the Father in this wonderful work He is doing in our time. Mattie takes a hard stand against fear and complacency in the church. He lives in Mobile with his wife, Candice, and their three sons Kai, Caleb, and Carver.